People,
Places
& Things

*A guide to
overcoming
addictive
behavior*

William W. Washington, Jr.

ELW Publications

People, Places & Things

A guide to overcoming addictive behavior

William W. Washington, Jr.

People, Places & Things

A guide to overcoming addictive behavior

©2008 William W. Washington, Jr.
2008941585
Library of Congress Control Number:

ISBN: 978-0-9766233-1-1
Design: Mickey Moore Design Associates
www.mickeymoore.com

ELW Publications

1831 SECRETARY'S ROAD • SCOTTSVILLE, VA 24590

Contents

GETTING STARTED

THE PITFALLS OF
PEOPLE, PLACES & THINGS

THE BENEFITS OF
PEOPLE, PLACES & THINGS

STAYING ON TRACK

Acknowledgments

To my wife, Joyce, there is so much that I can say. I look back on the years when my life was in turmoil and without direction; you went through seven years of hardship, but never gave up on the man you believed in. Because of your love and support, today I stand in victory in Christ Jesus. You have been a reflection of His life to me. I want to thank you from the deepest part of my heart for being the one whom I have very much needed. You are the "number two" in my life (Christ is number one), and I do believe that you're okay with that. I love you, Joyce.

I would also like to express my deepest appreciation and thanks to Jim and Diane Johnson, for your gracious encouragement and patience throughout the years we have known each other. You have supported me with the truth and restored me with your love.

To First Presbyterian Church in Charlottesville, again, I want to thank you for having faith in something you couldn't see. Because of that faith, many men and their families have received help through The Bridge. My wife and I have been strengthened by your encouragement in so many ways. Thanks for making a difference to us and to our community.

Dedication

When you dedicate a book, you look for someone who has made an impact on your life, who has proven to be a faithful friend. You look for someone who has been gracious through your difficult times, someone who has stood beside you because they believed in you and in what you were doing.

That's why I dedicate this book to John and Renee Grisham. The love and support you have given to our community, and also to my wife and me, have been above and beyond what I could have hoped for. As a result of your encouragement and the grace of God, The Bridge Ministry has been able to have an impact on many people. You have truly been an example of Christ's words to "love your neighbor as yourself." Thank you so much.

GETTING STARTED

INTRODUCTION:

A Way Out

If you're reading this book, chances are you have an addiction or know somebody who does. For these next few pages, I want you to try and forget most of what you know or think you know about addiction. I've got a few things to share with you that have changed my life and the lives of many others. I'm not proposing a new program or a quick fix. But what I have to share will, I believe, bring you great hope.

When we think about addiction, we usually focus on drugs and alcohol. My experience, both personally and in working with others, has been with drug and alcohol addictions. Still, you'll find that the principles in this book apply to many other addictions as well, because every addiction has the same end result: the power to control our lives and the lives of those around us, if we allow it.

Whatever the cause, however we got here, we

can find ourselves caught so firmly in addiction that we cannot find a way of escape. No matter how hard we try, we cannot achieve the goals we set for ourselves. Even worse, for all too many of us, addiction has separated us from those we love most.

It's not hard to see how addiction can bring us to a place like this. After repeated failures to "kick the habit," we simply submit to the behavior. After giving it our best, we give up and give in. We find ourselves cut off from those who love us—maybe because we didn't want to see them hurt any more, or because we got tired of listening to them, or because they became weary of trying to change us.

For a while at least, it almost seems easier to live this way—surrendered to addiction and cut off from people who care. But too many of us who have lived that way know otherwise. Eventually, the helplessness we feel slowly changes to hopelessness. It's almost as if we become paralyzed.

I've heard that if a bird has spent its whole life in a cage, it won't even move off its perch when the cage door is opened. It may have flown against that door a thousand times during its lifetime, hoping for a way out, but all of that effort wouldn't open the door. It seems to make more sense to stay where it is than to waste energy trying to do the impossible. So when the door is opened, the bird doesn't recognize it. You see, it's no longer the physical cage that keeps it frozen to the perch. Its own experience has become an even stronger cage.

That's the way it is with addiction, too. All of our efforts to escape our addiction have produced nothing. We have always gone back. The cage has stood firm, and we end up back where we started, or worse.

But I have some good news for you, news that at first you may find challenging to believe: If there was a way into it, there is a way out of it. Over the last seventeen years, I have learned to deal with addiction—in my own life and in the lives of others—not only through formal programs, but after the program is over. In fact, it's the "after"—when we're out on our own, so to speak—that is the most important part.

What's the key, you ask? It's so simple; you may have heard it before. It's expressed in three little words: people, places, and things.

The trick is not just to know it, but to live it. And that's what this small book is all about. I won't make a lot of easy promises here to tempt you to read on. There is a way out, but it won't be easy. The road may be straight, but that doesn't mean it won't test everything inside of you.

But if you feel like flying, come. The cage door is open.

GETTING STARTED

CHAPTER ONE

Where Do I Begin?

"Keep your room clean."

The young man standing across from me was looking a little confused.

"I was doing that before I came here."

"Okay," I said. "That's fine. Just keep your room clean here."

For the last seventeen years or so, I've worked with men who have problems with addiction. For close to ten of those years, the men's program I direct has included a place for these men to stay while they are a part of the program. That, of course, means that they've got a reasonable list of chores to keep up with, including taking care of their own rooms.

By the time men reach our program, they've often been through quite a few other options: various types of drug or alcohol detoxification, counseling, and perhaps jail. They have heard plenty of advice and received a lot of direction. In other words, they have not only done it all, they think they know it all.

And that's where a huge part of their problem lies.

When I first meet one of these men, he's typically got the routine down so well he wants to go through it all over again with me. He expects me to sit down and listen to all the trouble his addiction got him into, who and what he's lost, how he grew up, the tragedies he experienced at home. And almost always, he will be giving me a huge head-full of all the insights he's gained along the way.

But that's not what we need to talk about—at least not right away.

That's not saying that his problems aren't real, that the abuses he faced at home weren't terrifying, or that his losses haven't been painful. I know better than that. I've lived through it myself. But reciting his past isn't going to help him move forward. For all the wisdom of his insights—and you, too, would be impressed by them—they haven't gotten him anywhere but right where he is, and that's back to the beginning.

So, that's where we start. We begin with a simple, reachable goal. We go back to a simple place where a man can once again begin to find success. That's why I tell each one of them, "I want you to keep your room clean."

Bill, the young man in front of me that day, had been through three years of college, but it hadn't helped him beat his addiction. No matter how much he knew, his knowledge couldn't change him.

It actually insulted him that I asked him to start with something as simple as keeping his room clean and following a few rules. But at that point, I wasn't interested in his knowledge or his insights into his addiction. I wanted to help him get back to ground level, because that's where we needed to go to build the foundation. Unless we started there, with the basic structure and attitudes and character of his life, anything else we added would be in danger of falling apart. It's where each one of us has to go if we want to establish anything new and lasting in our lives.

Fix the Foundation

I have two friends who own a successful construction business. A few years ago, they were given the responsibility of renovating a mansion that was about a hundred years old. Outside, it showed all the markings of elegance and wealth: a beautifully crafted brick exterior, spacious old windows, and massive columns.

But that house had one very serious, very invisible flaw: The foundation on which it stood had not been properly laid.

No matter how skilled and careful the builders were, all of their renovations would soon show cracks and weaknesses, if built on a weak, crumbling foundation. So, before they started repositioning walls, shoring up floors, and realigning windows, they had to dig under the old foundation and build a new one. It was a muddy mess, and it sure didn't look like it had anything to do with making the house look better. But it had everything to do with making it last.

When a man comes into our program and I tell him, "I want you to keep your room clean," I'm giving him a stone for a new foundation. When I say, "You can only use the weight room between 4:30 p.m. and 5:30 p.m.," I'm giving him another stone for that foundation. Each stone is an important piece of restoring this man's life, but it's not obvious to him.

As I'm starting this process, more often than not a man will look at me with a puzzled expression.

"But what about my addiction?"

My response is, "Yes, I know. We'll get to that. Let's start by doing a few basic things."

To follow up, we do a room check every day. Over time, that room check will start revealing things about a person, things that point to areas of his foundation that still require some work. I remember once when Bill had some stuff in his room that he wasn't supposed to. It wasn't much: One time it was candy; another time it was a screwdriver that should have been put away with the other tools.

When we confronted him about these infractions, he had a simple answer: "I'm sorry. I wasn't aware of that rule." But I knew that wasn't true. We go over the rules and regulations every week. Bill was just trying to fall back on an excuse.

One day Bill was working in the kitchen at mealtime. All of the other men assigned to kitchen duty took a spot on the serving line, but Bill stood back.

"Why aren't you up there serving with the rest of the guys?" I asked.

"There's no room," came his unconvincing reply.

You might be thinking that these were not major issues, and that we were just "picking on him," as he suggested. Yet over and over we had heard these same kinds of excuses. It became obvious that these were not just occasional slip-ups. As Bill was required to live with the regularity of our schedule and responsibilities, old patterns of his life were becoming visible.

Making excuses was just the way Bill tried to avoid the truth about his behavior and deny the consequences of his actions. It was now our responsibility to hold him accountable. From time to time we took away some of his privileges to help him recognize the importance of his problem. That's when we saw his anger and an outright disrespect for leadership. It was clear we had touched something deep in his life.

Whether Bill's excuses were trying to protect an

old wound or the uncorrected behavior of his childhood, he had spent years adding layer after layer over the core problems in his life. That's why Bill had been locked into his addiction for so long. He had buried the pain and the patterns of behavior that fed the addiction.

The process of peeling back these layers takes time. Even after seventeen years or more of living successfully without a drug addiction, I still find these layers in my life.

For Bill, it wasn't until about six months after he began our program that things started to change. I had been encouraging the men to stop allowing their trials and challenges to "push them out of" their destiny, their purpose in life. Trials, I had been telling them, are there to show us what we need to overcome in order to reach our destiny, to show us that we are hopeless and helpless in our own strength. As I spoke, I could see Bill nodding his head as if he really understood.

The next day, he showed up at my office.

"Over the last few days, I've heard a lot of different things you've said that have challenged the lifestyle I've been living," he said. "But today, it made a real connection with me."

I knew he wasn't just saying those words to try and get some of his privileges back. It was obvious from the expression on his face that a light had come on somewhere inside. He had just needed some time to see a few of the patterns that had held him in bondage and not allowed him to live a productive life. Now that this was happening, we had something to build on.

In the process of asking him to keep his room clean and abide by the other rules, we had used physical boundaries to get to inner issues. As he was sitting there in front of me, I realized that what he didn't yet know—but would discover soon enough—was that those issues were deeper than I had been showing him. They were stronger than he could imagine.

"You have given up your life to serve this lifestyle of addiction," I told him. And he began to listen. "You have given up your career and your family."

Tears began streaming down his face. There was hurt and there were deep wounds—those he had inflicted and those he had received. It was a hard place for him to be, opening up this part of his life.

Afterward, I let the staff know what had happened, to prepare them for the process of "engagement." I could see that, for the next several weeks, Bill was going to go through a very tough time, and he would need a healthy balance of understanding and firmness. I knew that he'd be angry one minute; the next minute he would want to leave the program. It wouldn't be easy, but there were a lot of people supporting him, and if he'd choose to hang in, he'd come through stronger on the other side.

I see the same thing in many men in our program. Even as they *want* to change, they fight the process of healing. The pain and rejection is all tangled up inside of them like a big ball of yarn, and they feel defeated even thinking about it. Feeling overwhelmed, they want to run away from it all. But that response has just helped lock them up in their addiction. Because we are interested in helping them get through this process and successfully face these issues, they will also fight against us. They won't realize that they are really fighting against an outstretched hand ready to help.

Like so many others, Bill was just at the beginning of the process of change, but he wouldn't have been able to even get this far if we had not begun by slowly and carefully establishing a foundation, a place where he could experience some success.

It had really started with keeping his room clean. As he began to see the benefits of having order and structure in that one small part of his life, he gained encouragement that other aspects of his life could benefit from a similar change. That's why he came into my office that morning.

When Bill had first arrived, the structure had been a challenge. But as he embraced the structure in the little things and experienced success, it gave him the hope he needed—hope that would give him courage to address the bigger issues in his life. If we had tried to start with the big issues first, we would have been pushing Bill toward a familiar wall of defeat.

That's the hardship these men face as they go from program to program. Each time, they try to "take care of" what seems to be the obvious problem, the obstacle that has stopped them from growing— their addiction to drugs or alcohol. But these are only symptoms of deeper issues in their lives: rebellion, low self-esteem, anger. The list could go on and on.

With the beginnings of a foundation now in place in Bill's life, we could start adding knowledge and insight into some of the specific areas he was dealing with. But we were going to have to be careful there, too.

Watch Your Words

The right knowledge is important in overcoming our addictions, but sometimes people with addictive behavior will make an addiction out of knowing "the right things" to say. It's important to be able to take the knowledge we have and put it into practice.

We demonstrate what we really know and understand by how we act. If we've used a lot of words without backing them up with our actions, people may have learned not to pay too much attention to what we say. Our words really mean something to others when we follow through on what we say we are going to do.

When I was caught up in my own addiction, I remember promising myself and my family over and over again that I would quit. They weren't just words that I was using to get my wife to take some pressure off me. I was sincere and very serious. I was used to accomplishing what I set out to do. I had my own business, and—when I could make it to the job—I made good money. I was determined that overcoming my addiction would be just like everything else I had set my mind to do: I would just do it.

But when I couldn't keep that promise, it became clear that all my words and determination weren't making a difference. I hadn't changed, and I was convinced that I never would. It was one of the deepest sorrows I had ever known. And I let it bring me to a place of defeat and hopelessness.

One night as I walked through the door of our apartment, I looked at the woman I loved, asleep with our children. Each one was so precious to me. Why wasn't I able to provide for them the way I knew I was supposed to? The anger boiled up inside me. I was to blame for their suffering! I had tried my best, but I couldn't get out of the hole I was in, and I was dragging my family right down into it with me. How could I escape? How could I make it all just go away? Only one thing came to mind.

I tried taking my life that night. I took a handful of pills and inhaled as much gas as I could stand. I remember saying just before I passed out, "Thank God it's over."

But thank God it wasn't.

If you're at a place where death seems more precious than life, I want you to know something: Life has greater blessings in store for you than you could ever dream or imagine. I know from experience. Trust me: Your life is worth living all the way through. It's still true, though, that the failure of our words—our promises, our commitments, our goals—to produce lasting change can eventually bring us to a place of great despair and emptiness. It's obvious that words, even determined ones, cannot pull us out of the bondage of addiction. There's another important piece to the puzzle.

Quit the Con

Most every addict I know is a great con artist. They can lie and twist and turn their way through impossible situations and come out looking innocent and strong on the other side. But there's one person who's really getting the worst of the con game, and that's the con himself.

We tell ourselves that we are responsible workers,

but for some of us, a look at our employment history shows that we've lost six jobs in the last four years. We may be able to convince ourselves that we're good husbands and fathers, but some of us wonder why our families seem to keep their distance from us.

What we need—and what we're most afraid of having—is a "mirror," a true reflection of who we really are. But it's the first step each of us has to take.

The men in our program have other people around them who are willing to hold up "mirrors" for them until they are ready to do it for themselves. They are encouraged to be honest with each other, but they are also encouraged to speak the truth out of a deep concern and love for the other person. When we hear the truth from someone who really cares about us, it makes it easier to hear the hard things that we've tried so long to avoid.

Mirrors don't lie, but we can still walk away from a mirror and forget our true reflection. Some of the men in our program walk away from the truth by going back out on their own before they're ready.

Even if we're not in a program, many of us "walk away" from the truth every day by continuing to deceive ourselves. Some of us maintain the appearance that everything is "just fine," that our lives are in order. (Keep in mind, though, that whatever is going on *inside* of us will eventually show up on the *outside*.) Some of us try to hide behind our gifts and talents. We figure if people are impressed with what we can do, they won't get too close to asking hard questions about what we're really like. We take cover behind material possessions, which easily present the picture of "success." Or we may simply agree with our past defeats and convince ourselves that there is no way out of our situation—even that we were just "made" this way.

Whatever lies we believe, they usually hold us back from the important step of looking within ourselves to see the real issues we need to face. We develop the habit of blaming other people for things that have happened. What we're really doing is denying that we even have a problem. And that gives us an excuse for not having to make any changes.

It's no surprise, then, that a lot of men with addictions walk around with a "no one can tell me what to do" attitude. They can seem to be the picture of self-reliance and confidence—two character traits that are likely to draw others to them and even place them in positions of leadership.

But that attitude is not a sign of strength; it indicates a serious weakness. In fact, it is one of the most significant obstacles in our lives. That kind of attitude will not help us be successful or make us leaders. Real leaders have learned to listen to the truth, even when it points the finger at them.

If we convince ourselves that we don't need to listen to anyone, the only voice we hear is our own. We believe our own con game about who we are (who we imagine ourselves to be), and we are not aware of how foolish it makes us.

We have lived in lies and deceit for so long because we had hoped they would protect us. But even though our deepest needs and hurts may seem more hidden, they won't go away by covering them up. All our con game is doing is allowing our addictive patterns to grow deeper and stronger without our noticing them. But be sure of this: The consequences of our behavior will show up sooner or later, probably worse than we ever imagined.

Our freedom begins with being willing to listen to the truth. We almost certainly won't hear it all at once. That would be too much to deal with or to try to embrace. But we do need to hear the truth. First, we need to see ourselves as we really are. Then we can begin to become that person we were meant to be.

By now you're probably thinking, *How does all of this relate to people, places, and things?* I believe that to understand the truths in this book, we need to be honest with ourselves. Addictive lifestyles are not about honesty, so they keep us stuck in bondage. Honesty helps us get out of that bondage long enough to start building a foundation for a new life.

When I talk about people who understand the meaning of people, places, and things, I'm talking about those who have gone through a careful and deliberate process of building something in their lives. They are people who have started low, with humility and honesty, to lay a strong foundation. When they are prepared to graduate from a program such as ours and walk back into the community, that foundation supports them.

Structure is the first part of that foundation. It's what we seek to develop in our program when we tell a man to keep his room clean. It's what people do every day when they get up, go to work, and come home to friends and family. Structure is the consistency of having the right priorities. It establishes an order, putting things in place that have been out of place for too long. And structure has positive results. It gives us an example that life can be better, it leaves a place for hope to grow again, and it lays the foundation for our future growth.

With a good structure in place, we can learn to say no to our addiction from our heart, not just from our head. Our words will start to mean something, because we will be able to follow through with our actions. That's character: being dependable by saying we're going to do the right thing and then doing it.

As our words begin to mean something to us—as we live by the truth—we will find that the truth others have to tell us means something, too. We can have the courage to listen to people who care about us, to look in the mirror and begin to see ourselves as we really are. We become willing to be held accountable, to give other people permission to speak to us about uncomfortable issues. I don't know anyone who can beat addiction without honest accountability.

To summarize, then, where do we start in the battle against addiction?

• Fix the foundation—Build structure in your life slowly and patiently.

• Watch your words—Establish character by speaking and acting truthfully.

• Quit the con—Hold yourself accountable for your behavior, and let others hold you accountable.

There it is: structure, character, and accountability. Developing these, of course, is a process. This is not some "one-two-three" program with magic results. These are principles that we need to be working on constantly. We won't start today and arrive tomorrow. But if we don't start, we won't get out of the bondage we find ourselves in today.

As we engage in this process, we discover something crucial to winning the battle over our addiction: There are things in our lives deeper than the addiction itself. These are the hidden things that have been the fuel for the addiction, and they have done such a good job feeding that fire that we have been fooled into thinking that the addiction—the drugs or the drinking—was the main problem. But that's not true. The addiction is the *magnified* problem; it's the problem that has been around for so long it has become the excuse for not being productive, for our broken marriages, for not finishing college, and for all the other failures in our lives.

True, like any out-of-control fire, our addiction has caused a great deal of harm to us and to others. But if we focus on the addiction, we will never put out the flames. The fuel will still be there, ready to start the fire all over again.

The goal, then, is to discover what's been fueling our addiction. In the chapters to follow, we'll be looking for this fuel in three areas of our lives: people, places, and things. First, we'll examine how people, places, and things have been part of our problem, gaining insight into how we have gotten where we are today. Afterward, we'll take a look at how people, places, and things can become part of our solution to win the battle against our addictive behaviors.

We won't have the answers for everything, but that's okay. We don't have to be perfect to be successful; we just have to be honest about our addiction and the steps we need to take.

THE PITFALLS
OF PEOPLE, PLACES & THINGS

CHAPTER TWO:

With Friends Like You...

We don't have a choice about everyone who is going to be part of our lives, but we *can* choose our friends. Because of that, whom we choose as our friends says a lot about us. They will often share our interests and agree with us about what is important.

Sometimes our friends can be a reflection of our problems. For example, if we have an addiction, there's a good chance that at least some of our friends do, too. We're naturally more comfortable around people who won't be critical of the choices we make. But that doesn't mean we can blame our friends for our problems. Other people may tell us that, but if we're honest with ourselves, we know that our friends could just as easily blame us for *their* problems.

On the other hand, your friends may not share your problems at all. They may, in fact, be very different from you. They may have the kind of life you want to have, or that you imagine yourself having. Perhaps you admire them and want them to admire you, too. That's why you never let them see who you really are.

That's the mask we put on. If we are around people who have a stable life, a mask creates the impression that our own life is stable. Yet what we really need are honest relationships with others.

Even so, everyone tends to have at least a few close relationships. They may be governed by an unwritten code of loyalty, offering a strong sense of mutual support. When I was deep in my own addiction, I found strong loyalty even among drug dealers. You could count on a drug dealer to play by certain unspoken rules, at least up to a point. For one thing, they would agree on who was to be defended and who was to be attacked. Defending the group against a common enemy can provide a strong basis for support.

For those of us who have struggled with an addiction, an enemy can be anyone who challenges us to change. And that means that our "enemies" can come in all shapes, forms, and sizes.

Comfort Zones

Rick saw his family as his enemy because they started asking him questions about his addiction: "Why do you keep losing your job and doing drugs that are destroying your life? You need to get some help."

Rick wasn't ready to hear those kinds of questions, so of course he wasn't comfortable being around his family or anybody else who was trying to help him see his problem. Frankly, he wasn't convinced he *had* a problem. So he found a group of people who wouldn't ask questions. In other words, Rick found a "new family." They got high together, but no one talked about addiction or a need to change behavior. These new friends helped make his addiction "invisible." Rick was definitely more comfortable with this new group, but that just meant that he was in denial and didn't want to deal with the true issues in his life.

You may not be exactly like Rick. You may be aware—even painfully aware—that you have an addiction. But every time you've tried to get free, you've lost the battle. Facing your addiction means facing the probability of another defeat, and you've told yourself that it would hurt too much to try again.

Eventually, you may have ended up in a group where your addiction seemed invisible. It may seem more comfortable there, but these people may be giving you false encouragement. In the meantime, your invisible addiction has breathing room to grow stronger and stronger. The stronger it becomes, the more defeated *you* become.

Groups like this can also mask an addiction

that's just developing. Take Jamie, for example. Jamie was in high school when he discovered that smoking marijuana seemed to help him play the drums better. Because he was around a group of people who were also doing drugs, what he was doing seemed pretty normal. Besides, none of his friends looked like they were getting in serious trouble.

Every day just before band, he would get high. The success he felt with his music encouraged him to use the drug more often, not just before band, but whenever he wanted to relax. So far, it seemed like this was good, that things were working out in his favor. His music seemed to be better, and he believed that he was overcoming some of his nervousness around girls and developing confidence in other areas.

After high school, Jamie's friends moved on with their lives, some going to college, others to jobs. But Jamie was stuck. Marijuana led to other drugs. He never graduated, never was able to hold a job for very long. Relationships suffered, and ironically, he hardly thought about the drums. Even his gift of music had been sacrificed to his addiction. What he had originally thought was the answer to building his self-esteem had now put him in a lifestyle of bondage. His low self-esteem was still there; he had only added to his problems.

Jamie's situation is not unusual. As long as

enough people around us are engaged in the same behavior, or as long as they accept our behavior or refuse to challenge us to change, it's easy to fool ourselves into believing that everything is fine. *My behavior isn't that much worse than everyone else's*, we think. It's possible for us not to realize what's happened until it's too late, when everyone else is moving forward and we're still stuck in our addiction so deep we can't figure out how we got there, much less how to get out.

Caught up in the addiction, our lives become completely out of control. The addiction becomes our life, and it controls us. It will steal our career, our family, our hope. It can destroy everything we've worked for. As Jamie found out, what started as a casual habit can quietly become a controlling force. What a young boy thought was a way to improve his musical ability became the means to rob him of that ability and of so much more.

Life in the Crab Pot

It's easy to get caught up in addiction because it's not something that always comes initially packaged with a red "warning" light. We might see warning signs along the way. But often, it's only when the pain of living with our addiction becomes serious enough that we try to get out.

Some of us have tried going to programs that train our minds to overcome the addiction. They teach us to say or "know" the right things— assuming that information and insight will enable us to find our own way out.

But that's just not enough. True, knowledge may be part of the solution, but addiction is so deep-rooted that it becomes a part of your life and your soul. If it has taken fifteen years of bondage for you to get where you are today, it's going to take some time to learn how to get out of your addiction, and to put boundaries around yourself to help you make it through to a life of freedom.

You can have your life back, but it's not going to be easy. It's going to take commitment to walk through the challenges and hardships that will face you. It's going to take endurance and sacrifice. But it will be worth it. It will be worth all the difficulties, because what awaits you is the joy of being free to really enjoy your life, the peace that comes from living with a healthy structure, and the hope of a more secure future.

But even after we've made the decision to get out, we've got another problem as serious as the addiction itself. In fact, it's been a big part of our addiction all along: the group of people we have associated with.

Those in our group who are still caught in the bondage of addiction don't want us to get free. If there's a way out for us, it opens up the possibility that there's a way out for them, too. For many of them, that's not something they're interested in, because it will require them to take a serious look at their own problems. Some of them may not believe it's possible for them to change. Or, like Jamie, they may not even realize they have a problem. If they never get out of their addiction, it just confirms what they've been thinking all along: *This is the way it has to be.* Though it may be hard to believe, some addicts enjoy their lifestyle and don't want to be set free from it.

The relationship addicts have with each other reminds me of a time when I was watching some people catch crabs. One of the most common ways to catch crabs is to put some bait in a wire mesh cage called a "crab pot." Each side of the crab pot has an opening through which it's easy for the crabs to enter but almost impossible for them to escape.

So far, you can probably see how fishing for crabs is a lot like addiction: The crabs wander in, thinking that there is something good for all of them in the crab pot. More and more of them arrive, drawn toward the bait. Each is unaware of the danger until it's too late, when they're caught and eventually pulled up out of the water.

But here's what really caught my eye: When the fisherman opens the crab pot and any one of the crabs finally has an opportunity to get out, not a single one escapes. The crabs are so busy attacking one another, holding each other in their grasp, that they are just one big tangled mess. No one crab can get free.

Many of us have felt as if we have gotten "free" of our addictions only to have them come back with a vengeance, and there have been people in our lives who have encouraged that. Like crabs in a pot, they are holding on to us with all their strength. It may be an old saying that "misery loves company," but there's a lot of truth to it. And misery has claws.

Family Matters

It may surprise you to know that our families can act like the crabs in a crab pot.

For some of us, our family has been our best support system. They have pushed us to get help, and when they do start to see some change in our lives, they are there to encourage us all the more.

For others, our family has been part of the problem. If you're not sure how that could be, let me ask you a question: How can someone with a serious addiction continue to get by for so long and never face serious consequences?

It just might be because he has an unhealthy support system. His wife may call in sick for him. She may even have a job that pays the bills. His children, too ashamed or too afraid to bring friends over to the house, do their part by helping to limit outside contact with the family. Everyone walks on eggshells to avoid facing the anger that seems to spill out unpredictably. No one talks about the problem. Just like the group of "friends" we talked about before, all of the family's efforts make the addiction "invisible."

The addiction we have is more than just the object of our addiction, such as drugs, alcohol, or pornography. As we've pointed out, the real addiction is the behavior we have allowed to take root in our lives. And our families are often part of that addiction.

Jim's mother saw that the group Jim was hanging around with really weren't his friends. They were only interested in using him. When Jim didn't have any money to buy their drugs or a car to take them places, his "friends" were nowhere to be found.

But his mother was. If Jim needed to get somewhere, his mother would drive him. If he was in need of some extra money, she would give it to him. All along she thought she was supporting her son and trying to help him; she later realized she was just enabling him to avoid the consequences of his behavior. The transportation she offered and the way she helped him get out of financial difficulties was just the cushion he needed to stay comfortable with his addiction.

In these ways and others, families can become part of the problem. Just like the addict, their lives are controlled by the addiction and the behaviors that feed it, and they don't have the answers. That's why they, too, sometimes stop asking the questions. They end up denying the reality of the addiction by trying to eliminate its natural consequences.

The consequences, painful as they are—going to jail, losing a home or a family, being deeply in debt, etc.—can bring an addict to a place of healing. If every time an addict gets close to being in a difficult place he has someone to bail him out, he can never begin the process of healing. An addict must see himself and the consequences of his actions for what they really are, before he can take steps to move away from his lifestyle of addiction.

A good family is built on love and support, but an addiction drains the family of those things. By the time a parent or spouse draws the line with the addict and finally says, "No more," there's a strong chance that the love and support is not as strong as it once was, because that addiction has robbed so much of the good things that family had to give. And, sometimes, at the end of that road there can be dead relationships.

The examples that encouraged your addictive behavior may have even come from within your own family. More than one man in our program has told me that he followed the examples of a father, a mother, a brother, or a cousin. Somehow, because they were family, the addiction seemed "safer"—even approved.

Family is meant to be a place of security, a place where we learn the right things to do. When addictive patterns in our family become our examples, that lifestyle creates confusion. Being part of a dysfunctional family doesn't give us a lifelong excuse, but it can help us realize what a challenge it can be to understand and follow the right path.

Both of my parents were alcoholics, and just like any other kid growing up in that kind of home, I became a part of the addictive pattern without even realizing it. More than that, the addictive pattern became part of me. Long before my dad gave me my first bag of marijuana when I was ten—to show his love for me, he thought—I was already living an addictive lifestyle.

What do I mean by that? The bonds of family are strong bonds, and they pull every member of the family in one direction or the other. We may say, "I'll never be like my father," but that will be a difficult promise to keep. I don't believe in fate— that just because you grew up in a family where there was addictive behavior, you will become an addict too. But childhood examples do exert a strong influence. In order to see change in your own life, you have to deliberately and persistently walk a different way. And, as much as you might want to, you can't do it alone.

Sometimes our families can become the biggest challenge for us when we decide to change. In fact, they are often the trap that we walk blindly back into. I don't mean that you should abandon your family—far from it! I'm a strong believer in doing everything you can to provide for your family and to take care of them. But it's important to be aware that certain patterns in your family that you have been part of—maybe even helped to establish—will trip you up over and over again unless you are aware of them and make a definite change of course.

Hard Choices

Family means a lot to me, including my extended family of cousins and uncles. My father had four brothers, so we have a pretty large family. I live about an hour away from them, but I have to tell you, I haven't seen most of them in the last ten years. It has been my choice, but it wasn't an easy choice.

After my life changed from being a drug addict and dealer to someone who had hope and purpose, I really wanted to share that hope with others. Of course, the first people who came to mind were my own family. My wife, Joyce, had walked away from her old lifestyle, and we were seeing the change in our children, but I wondered about my family back home. Who would tell them that there was a way out?

Joyce, like many wives, has a good understanding of her husband. She had told me repeatedly to stay away from my family, but I refused to listen. I was going with a good heart, I told myself. I was going to help them. But Joyce was right: Once I was with them, within an hour I was doing all the things from which I had been set free.

That was many years ago. I came back to my wife, broken and defeated. (One of my cousins had actually put me in his truck and driven me home. Even he knew I shouldn't have been there.) That's probably when I first began to get a glimpse of the difficult but important lessons of people, places, and things—the understanding that the long-established patterns of our lives are really what feed our addiction.

It's especially hard when the people you're trying to separate from know intimate things, secrets, about you. I have a cousin who had watched me take advantage of my family when I was drinking and drugging; he had watched me spend my paycheck on drugs while my wife and children went hungry. He had also seen the violence in my life. Because he was a reminder of my past, he was a difficult person for me to deal with. He was the one always saying—with his attitude as much as with his words—"You know you haven't changed!"

Another close relative of mine is much the same way. A few years ago, he was helping me with a job outside my house. By that time in my life I had spent more than ten years leading a men's program that helped other people with addictions. He could see that my life had changed and that I was persistent in the way that I was living, that my family was happy. He could see that I was taking care of my family's needs. I had been telling him about some of the amazing changes that had taken place in my life. Then he looked straight at me and asked with a gleam in his eye, "You're still getting high every now and then, aren't you?"

There will always be those difficult people who challenge the fact that our lives changed. They may not want us to change, or they just might not be able to believe that it's possible. That can be discouraging, and their words and attitudes can encourage us to withdraw from people. That's a way that a lot of us have lived.

Solitary

Not every person who struggles with addiction goes where the crowd goes. Not all of us do our drinking or drugging with friends. Sometimes, because of shame or a fear of being discovered, we engage in the object of our addiction in a "secret" place, by ourselves.

If you're one of those people, you should know

that no matter how you are trying to hide it, your addiction is affecting others. No one drinks alone. No one watches pornography alone. Rather, all of our addictive behaviors have an effect on someone else. Despite our best efforts, we are still connected to other people.

You may not understand it, but that's what drove me to attempt to take my life that night. I had come to the conclusion that no matter how I tried to hide my addiction, I was hurting the people I said I loved.

You see, I had tried desperately to protect my family from the lifestyle of my addiction. If I was high, I wouldn't come around my family, since my lifestyle would have brought a dangerous environment of people, places, and things into my home. Sometimes I'd be gone for days, but even then, my addiction was taking its toll on those who cared about me, my wife and my children who missed me.

If nothing else, just the fact that I was gone affected them. I know my wife worried about me, and so did my children, even though they were young. All the money and time that I wasted on drugs was not available to help meet my family's needs.

Also, when I was high, I didn't want to communicate with Joyce or my kids. If she ever challenged me about my drug use, I would respond with anger and frustration. And when the addiction was completely out of control, I would encourage Joyce to become a part of the lifestyle I was living. That way, she would not challenge my addiction and I could continue doing the things I wanted to do.

You may think you're leaving your addictive behaviors somewhere else, but believe me, they are so much a part of the way you live and act that you take those patterns with you wherever you go. Perhaps you think you have a "secret" addiction, but it will still have effects on you and others around you. You may have a "few beers" by yourself somewhere, but even if you're not around anyone else until you're sober, your lifestyle is affecting those around you.

Again, it's not just the addiction that we're talking about. It's the life-controlling behaviors that feed the addiction. These are the deeper, hidden problems. You're trying to deceive those who care about you. You're hiding a part of you that needs healing. And all of those behaviors have an effect on your relationships.

I'm thankful that Joyce was aware of how much the drugs were affecting my life and how much I needed help. As for me, I was in denial, and my life was out of control. The reality of my problem was too much for me to embrace.

You may be feeling the same way. That's why

you've tried to go into hiding with your addiction. Maybe hiding has even seemed to work for a while. But, again, negative consequences from these patterns in your life will show up sooner or later. My guess is that they may have already shown up; you just haven't been able to see them. Or maybe you have seen them and chosen to ignore them. You've gotten used to them, like a man living with a limp that he doesn't believe can be cured. He thinks he has exhausted all the possibilities, been to all the doctors. Everyone around you has gotten used to that limp, too. They've just accepted it along with you.

I see this happen all the time. A man will come to me and tell me that he's already been through a drug program, and it didn't work. He's convinced that there's no hope in trying that again. This man has tried many different answers, many different programs. But because he's been through so much with so little success, everyone around him has accepted defeat with him.

But don't lose hope. The man who is living in defeat hasn't yet been exposed to the right answer: the right people, places, and things. Change is possible, no matter how long you have lived like that. I want you to see the possibility of change in your life, and to hold on to a hope that will not disappoint you.

Of course, change doesn't come about by

continuing to hide. It starts with the truth, by bringing things out in the open, by finding someone to trust with the things that are so hard to be honest about. We have all kinds of ways of encouraging people to keep their distance. We can be annoying or withdrawn. We can try to come up with quick little jokes that make people laugh and (we hope) like us, but which don't really encourage a deep conversation. Some people use sarcasm, since if they're always acting like a smart aleck, other people have no reason to take them seriously. And it doesn't take long for these habits to become part of our personality. People begin to think of us as someone they can never really get close to, so that it seems we really are alone.

Yet, whether we admit it or not, we're never alone. Recognizing that my life was connected to others was one of the things that led me to an awareness of my own addiction. My hope is that leaving a life of secrecy and finding people who care will become the first step in your healing, too.

Starved for Praise

When you find people who care about you, they can strengthen your hope for change. When these people see you doing well, they will want to encourage you.

I always look for opportunities to encourage the men in our program. If I see them successful at something, even if it's a little thing, I want to let them know that they're on the right track. We all need a little bit of hope.

Sometimes, however, even the people who care about us won't give us the right kind of encouragement.

What do I mean? We have become such experts at deceiving ourselves and others to get what we want, we even know how to get praise when we need it. We can put on such a good front that people will praise us for the image we're creating instead of for any real change in our lives.

Frank was a man in our program who was gifted in many ways. He talked about starting a program of his own one day, but when I looked closely at his life, I could see that there were things that needed to be changed before he could become the leader he wanted to be. He hadn't yet learned to put into practice the things he had learned in the program. That was going to take time.

One night I took the men in the program to a meeting where the other people present were not aware of the challenges these men faced as a result of their addictive behavior. As Frank spoke, most of these people began to see how obviously gifted he was, how passionate he felt about seeking change in his life and in the lives of others. So, naturally, they encouraged him and gave him quite a lot of praise.

What they didn't know was that, just a few weeks earlier, I had taken this young man back to court. Frank had agreed to be in our program as an alternative to a jail sentence, but after several months with us, his strong negative attitudes were causing problems for the other men around him. Often, the last step before I dismiss a man from our program is to take him back before the judge who has sentenced him. Even the night of the meeting I'm talking about, it wasn't clear to me that Frank was going to finish the program.

It's typical for men who come into our program to blame other people and situations for their problems. If they can just stop that and start looking within themselves for the problems, they can experience deep change. But because Frank continued to try to "fix" everything and everyone else but himself, he was still struggling with the same issues that brought him to us in the first place—not the addiction itself, but the people, places, and things that fueled the addiction.

As a result, the praise Frank received that night didn't produce the encouragement that it was intended to give. Instead, it made him feel that he was above the rest of the men, that somehow he didn't have to do everything like everyone else had to do. He took the liberty of going off on his own instead of following the assigned schedule while we were there at the meeting. It was a little thing really, but it said a whole lot.

When I confronted Frank about his actions, he was apologetic, but his apology didn't touch the heart of the issue. He had allowed himself to be built up in pride, and pride can blind us to the truth. (You don't necessarily see the results of pride immediately, but sooner or later you will.) There may be several people in your life who build your ego through compliments and praise. There's nothing wrong with a well-placed compliment, but it can sometimes become fuel for the fire of addictive behaviors.

The problem is that those of us with life-controlling issues often have such low self-esteem we are starved for compliments. I think Frank may have been talking about the importance of change in his own life and about eventually starting his own program for men with addictions because he knew it was the kind of talk that would make him feel accepted in the group that night. It would make him feel like he was "somebody."

What he failed to realize is that it is not the exterior that brings change, but dealing with the issues within, issues such as hurt, pain, and rebellion. These have to be confronted before they destroy everything that has been built in our lives. Though having a program of his own may be a real desire—even a calling—in Frank's life, it will require a lot more than talk to see it established and sustained.

Listening to Others

You may be reading this book and not even realize you have a problem with addiction. Or, you may realize it, but you believe you're getting along just fine; your life isn't out of control.

When the arguments and fights come, as far as you're concerned, they come out of nowhere, for no good reason. *What's their problem?* you think. Actually, that attitude is a big part of the problem. We can become so occupied looking outside ourselves to place the blame somewhere else, that we can't see what's going on inside.

My wife, Joyce, taught a class in our program. After she finished, she remarked, "If the men would only allow themselves to hear what they are saying to each other, they wouldn't even need us."

The insights and wisdom she heard in the meeting were the same truths she was trying to present. But while the men may listen to something from one of the leaders, they are often not willing to hear the same thing from other people who are struggling with an addiction themselves.

And I understand why. They have heard a lot of other people with life-controlling issues and addictions talk about success and freedom, but they haven't seen them walk it out.

We can also ignore what others say because we are more interested in teaching than in being taught. That's just another way to avoid our own issues. As long as our main goal is to change others, we can more easily hide from our own addiction.

Through the patterns of our addictive lifestyle, we can use people as excuses for our behavior or as targets for our criticism instead of seeking them for answers. We can take even the positive relationships in our lives and make something negative out of them through criticism and faultfinding.

It's clear we have to see change in our relationships with people in order to get free and stay free of our addiction. I guarantee you that it's possible. We'll talk more about that in the second half of the book.

Meanwhile, let's take a look at something else that's been feeding our addiction: the places we've been.

THE PITFALLS
OF PEOPLE, PLACES & THINGS

CHAPTER THREE:

Off-Limits Places

Just like the people we spend time with, the places we go can have a powerful influence. For those of us who have struggled with an addiction, there are several obviously wrong places to be. Your list of places will be different from mine, but we can all point to several places we've been that we know have only encouraged us in our addiction.

In our men's program, we talk about those places and the effect they have had on us. But I'm not so concerned that the men in our program will head back to those obviously wrong places like a bar or a wild party—at least not at first. What I'm more concerned about are the other places, the hidden traps that they don't realize are a part of their addiction. They may not be places where the object of their addiction is even present, but they can still be places that can feed their addictive patterns and often lead back to the drug or alcohol.

There are a lot of places like that in our lives—

places associated with our old friends and just having a "good time," such as a popular neighborhood hangout or a favorite vacation spot. Other places might seem okay at first. After a while, however, we find them triggering our addiction. An example might be a local restaurant where beer is served, or the home of someone we admire who makes questionable choices in the movies and magazines he keeps in his home. Wherever they are, it's safe to say that the places that trigger our addiction are often *familiar* places.

Institutionalized Neighborhoods

In familiar places, we find it more difficult to even *see* the destructive patterns that feed our addiction, much less try to break free from them.

Take, for example, the most familiar place you can imagine. It may even be your home. There, you know the patterns of the people around you. You know how they have helped cover up for you, or how you may have fooled them. You know the places where you hid your drugs or alcohol or magazines. You've got a memory full of excuses, arguments, lies, broken promises, and lost dreams. For these reasons, your home may be the hardest place you could ever choose to get on a new track, to finally break free from your addiction.

What may seem innocent for the moment can put us back in the same place and mindset we have fought so hard to get out of. Before we realize it, we find ourselves back in the same addiction.

For many of us, it's not just our home or our family that provides that familiar environment; it's our entire neighborhood or community. My wife, Joyce, grew up in a neighborhood that was filled with people who could trace their connection to poverty, drinking, and drugs back through several generations. It wasn't a lifestyle for them; it went deeper than that. It was all they knew and all many of them could ever imagine.

I grew up in a similar environment. If you've read my story in the book *His Grace Is Sufficient*, you know what I'm talking about. Violence was a way of life where I lived. I saw people brutally hurt on a regular basis. My community was a place where some people were born in bondage, lived in bondage, and died in bondage. For me, it was also home. And because it was home, I grew comfortable there.

Don't get me wrong. There were plenty of times when I was very much afraid, and I lived with a nearly constant, almost silent fear of my father's anger. But it was all so familiar to me, because I had never known anything else. Just like a lot of the people in Joyce's old neighborhood, I had no idea there could be anything different.

When I was in prison, I even found a sort of contentment behind those bars. I gradually developed a feeling of security. I got used to the routine, appreciated the regular schedule, and grew comfortable getting meals that I didn't have to worry about providing. I even had a welcome break from the terrors of crack cocaine. I had a lot of reasons to grow content with my situation. The ironic thing was that this place of contentment was also my place of confinement.

When I got out of prison, I discovered that the prison I carried around inside myself had even stronger bars. It was a prison of familiar people, places, and things. Even though this internal prison held my hurts, my anger, and my resentments, it was all so familiar, I still easily fell back into it. Again, it was a place of contentment that was also my place of confinement.

We sometimes describe people who have been in jail over and over again as "institutionalized." The dictionary describes a person who is institutionalized as someone who has become "apathetic [unemotional, unmotivated] and dependent after a long period in an institution"—in other words, people who get used to the environment and the routine. In fact, they may feel lost without it, so of course they are not seeking to change it. That's true of a lot of people who are in jail today, and it was certainly part of my story.

But I believe that institutionalization starts long before the individual goes to jail even the first time. Institutionalization begins in our communities, in our neighborhoods, and in our families. It starts with patterns that have been handed down sometimes for generations: ways of mistreating those we say we love, irresponsibility to our commitments, treating discipline and boundaries like they are our jailers instead of our safeguards. Those traditions—and they include our patterns of addiction—are the real beginnings of institutionalization.

Let me say it again: The places where we are comfortable can be places of great danger for us. We need to wake up! We have grown comfortable in our bondage. Bondage that lives within our thinking and within our hearts will sooner or later make itself obvious to those around us.

In effect, we are in prison to a lifestyle, not only because of how we grew up, but also because of how we have responded to those patterns. I remember coming back before a judge for a second time on the same offense. The state prosecutor looked at me and said, "I don't understand. We gave you a chance to be free."

I wanted to tell him, "You didn't give me a chance to be free. You gave me an opportunity to go back out and do the same thing again."

Letting me out of jail hadn't set me free. I was still imprisoned because of my patterns of thinking and living. When we carry our prison around inside of us, we will always be in bondage. And that prison will be a part of our lives every day, whether we are in jail or out of jail.

What we need is a vision for something different, and it has to come from outside of the prison, from outside of the expectations and habits and patterns that have lured us into bondage. A lot of people get hope by looking at my life, or at other individuals who have broken free of their addiction. For some, even that isn't enough.

An Issue of the Heart

Sterling was a man who had been in our program for about two-and-a-half years. While there, he saw an example of a real community of caring people. He was loved and accepted, even with his problems. He was told the truth, but he heard it in such a way that he knew we were trying to help him, not just point out his old wounds. And for a while, he experienced a certain freedom from his addiction. We were able to get him a job, and he was amazed by the trust placed in him. He began to make some good friends, friends who truly cared about him and supported him. He acted as a leader to other men who were seeking freedom from their own addictions.

From our perspective, we believed we had reached some significant areas in his life that had held him in bondage. And then, Sterling just went back to a familiar place, a place from which he had been set free. He returned to his old lifestyle of addiction. For a while, he had acted like he was free from his past, but there was some place in his heart still living in captivity to the old ways.

At some point, you have to believe in your heart that you don't need to live in the old patterns anymore. What Sterling was doing—even though it was positive from outward appearances—was somehow not fully connected to his heart. He had learned the language of freedom; he had even acted in the role of a leader, but his heart wasn't free. It had deceived him and us. It's true that the heart is more deceitful than anything we can imagine.

That's why the program I direct focuses on the behavior and not the addiction. Addiction is just an outward sign of the problems that lie in our heart, in the deepest part of who we are as people. To even have a chance at ending the addiction, each of us needs to address our past hurts and failures, and the things that have brought us shame. If we focus on the addiction and neglect the issues of the heart—all of which tie into our behavior—we may find help to stay away from the object of our addiction for a few weeks or months, but that's about it. Our hearts are great at clouding the real issue. In fact, they are great at convincing us that we don't even have a problem, because they give us something "better": an excuse to cover up our behavior.

The Thirty-Eight-Year-Old Excuse

There is a very old story about a man who couldn't walk. He lived in the ancient city of Jerusalem, where they put men in his condition at a place locally known as the House of Mercy. He lived there with a lot of other people like himself: some who could not walk, perhaps others who could not hear or see. Some likely were missing arms or otherwise disfigured by an injury.

This particular man had lived there among these other sick, disfigured, and hurting people for thirty-eight years. For thirty-eight years he had seen people continue to be sent here, and everyone he saw leave was carried out as a corpse—well, almost everyone. You see, not far from the place where he lay on his mat was a pool of water. It was said that every so often an angel would come down and stir the water. Then, the first person to get into the pool would be healed. Evidently this had happened more than once, but in thirty-eight years it had not happened to this man.

As he explained it: "No one is ever here to help me get into the water. Someone else always gets in before I do."

The hope available to this man—that he might

someday be first into the pool—should have motivated him to do something about his condition. Instead, it became the focus of his discouragement. It became a tool to defeat him even more.

Do you see what I mean? A place that should have been uncomfortable became, in a way, comfortable. He had lain there for thirty-eight years. I would think that in that amount of time, seeing so many others healed, he would have figured out a strategy to get to the water. When family members or friends visited, or as people came by to give him alms, he could have asked them to move him closer to the edge of the pool. At the very least, perhaps, he could have crawled close enough to the edge to roll in when the waters were stirred. Even with his handicap, he could have moved an inch or two every day. I don't know, but I find it hard to believe that in thirty-eight years he couldn't have done something a little more than make excuses. But he was not looking for a way out; he was looking for comfort.

But what about our own lives? Where have we been stuck for years and years and years with nothing more than an excuse?

My father was an alcoholic.

Neither of my parents cared about me.

I didn't have a good example to follow.

I was abused and have always been looking for love.

And on and on. The places that we're stuck are not always physical places. They can be emotions, reasons, or rationalizations. But we are no different from that lame man lying in the House of Mercy. We are stuck on an excuse that leaves us defeated, an excuse that takes away all hope and leaves us with no desire to try to change our lives.

My own life is full of potential excuses. My father shot me when I was fourteen years old, and I ran away from home shortly afterward. Though I had loved him—and he, in his own way, had loved me, too—he had physically abused and threatened me more times than I want to remember. The pain of that experience was almost impossible for me to face. For other people looking at my life, it may have seemed as if I had a good "reason" for my addiction. But thank God I didn't hold on to that pain as my excuse. If I had, I would have held on to my addiction, too, and I'm sure that would have killed me.

An excuse can become a comfortable place, a familiar place we go in order to get out of our responsibility to change and grow.

I know a young man named Charlie who's not so young anymore. He's spent some time in jail as a result of his addiction, and he's been in some other trouble, too. The first time I met Charlie, he looked straight at me and said, "My father left me when I was eleven years old."

Charlie's life has been stuck on his past hurt for about twenty years now, because he has used the pain from the rejection of his father to excuse his wrong actions and bad decisions ever since. It's not necessarily true that he has been looking for an excuse. It could be that the pain is so overwhelming that he doesn't know how to deal with it. But as long as he continues to hold on to his past hurts, he'll find it hard to move forward. Now well into his adult life, Charlie has not been able to hold a job, he's had many broken relationships, and as I've already mentioned, he's been in trouble with the law.

One day I looked at Charlie and said, "You may not like what I'm going to say, but it's time for you to take responsibility for today."

A lot of men who come into our program say, "You don't understand. You just can't understand what I've been through."

Even though I may have been through similar circumstances, it's true that I still won't understand everything you've gone through. But what I do understand is that you can't continue to be stuck from something that happened to you twenty years ago. You have to make a decision about your life and when you're going to start living it again.

Otherwise, you'll stay right where you are. Is that what you really want? Of course it isn't, not if you've come to understand the truth: Your addiction and the behaviors that feed it are stealing your life.

We may have been given disadvantages in our lives, obstacles that have discouraged us, that have seemed impossible to overcome. But they cannot become our excuses. Yes, it will take persistence to overcome these obstacles, but there is a freedom—a healing—available for your life as you start putting the principles of this book into practice.

The Environment of Addiction

We learned from the crippled man in the House of Mercy that we can hold onto excuses for a very long time. But there's something else we need to learn from his story.

He was not alone.

All around him sat people who were sick and injured for one reason or another. They could have received their wounds in a war or in an accident at work. Perhaps some had been born with physical challenges. People who were once part of an active, lively society were now living on the fringes of that society. Now they were part of a society of sick people.

It's not unusual for people with addictions to find themselves in a similar place. As we've talked about, that environment may be the neighborhood we grew up in or live in today. But there's more. Our addictive lifestyle can actually help *create* an environment that encourages our addiction. It's hard to see, though, because as I've said earlier, we tend to associate with people who are just like us, people who deny their addiction. And if we deny our addiction, it's that much easier to deny the environment we're living in.

If we are living an addictive lifestyle, we're living in a society of sick people, people who need healing. This society helps keep the addiction alive, because it holds so many reminders of our addiction.

A man who is addicted to alcohol can be tempted to go back to drinking just by seeing a wine bottle. If just a single bottle can have that strong an effect, imagine what an entire environment can do. Your own environment is a place in which you've lived for a while now. It's a place you're used to. You've learned its unspoken rules. Your addiction has become part of your everyday choices, thoughts, and feelings. Your bondage is associated with the people you are with, the places you go, and the things you do—people, places, and things.

I know that some of us don't have the resources to leave the environment we're in. I was one of them. When I first began walking away from my addiction, I had to return to a place where drug dealers lived right up the street. I couldn't leave my environment, so I had to make some changes in the way I dealt with it. Each of us has to learn to see what is affecting us in our own environments and put boundaries in our lives. And in terms of boundaries, know this: There can be no gray areas. Your boundaries need to be clearly cut, black and white. If you start walking into the gray areas, making excuses and justifying your behavior, you will find yourself in a vulnerable place.

You're probably at least going to have to stay away from certain places in your environment where the bonds of addiction have been strong. You're going to have to separate from people who don't want to be part of something good and wholesome, who won't leave their old lifestyle.

Your choices begin today. You need to decide today what direction you want to go. Do you want life and freedom? Or do you want to stay in your place of bondage?

Some of you might actually need to leave your familiar environment for a while. That's a hard choice to make, and for some, it's made *for* us through a jail sentence or some other harsh consequence of our behavior, like divorce or a broken family.

Don't wait for those kinds of negative consequences to push you out of your environment. Make a choice now to seek real change in your life. Because if you don't, even if you leave the present environment of your bondage, you'll take that same environment with you because it's a part of who you are. Again, as long as you let the addictive behavior continue to live within you, sooner or later it will create that old, familiar environment around you. You'll find the dealer, the liquor store, the pornography—and you'll find the people to be a part of that environment.

We can always try to use our environment as just another excuse, just another way to stay where we are. The truth is that neither our environment nor the people in our environment made our bad choices for us. For whatever reason we've found ourselves in this addictive lifestyle, we need to hear it again: If there was a way in, there is a way out. But it's going to take a lot more strength than we have on our own. If you haven't seen that in the examples I've given so far, I believe the next chapter will help open your eyes a little more.

THE PITFALLS
OF PEOPLE, PLACES & THINGS

CHAPTER FOUR:

Things In Our Way

Just as there are familiar people and places in our lives that can fuel our addiction, there are also many things that can help keep us trapped in patterns of destructive behavior.

As I mentioned in the last chapter, for some alcoholics, just seeing a wine bottle can trigger a return to the object of the addiction. I'm sure you can name a few things that work the same way for you: a crack pipe, a certain television ad, the magazine rack at the grocery store. These are the negative things in our lives that obviously can have a bad effect.

But what about the positive things, the things that people say are part of enjoying success and the good life? Have they contributed to our addiction, too?

The Not-So-Good Life

The first time I met Gary, he seemed like a nice,

well-mannered young man. Though he had come to our program in need of help, he had a lot of things going for him that most of the men did not. He had grown up in a wealthy, relatively stable family. Though Gary had not suffered from the brokenness and poverty many of the other men had known, he had suffered in at least one way that even he wasn't aware of: He was used to getting what he wanted, when he wanted it, and how he wanted it. Getting new things became a familiar way of trying to escape his negative feelings and make himself happy.

It was no surprise that when Gary developed a serious addiction, he used his ability to buy new things as a cover-up for that addiction. Even though he was hanging around drug addicts, he still wanted to be accepted by his old friends who weren't addicted. Buying things was not only an attempt to stay on good terms with those friends, but it also gave him the feeling that everything was still basically okay. Sure, he was doing drugs, but nothing had really changed, and all this new stuff proved it, he convinced himself. When he bought a new car, it made him feel really great—at least for the first few months. After that, he just felt empty inside. Gary bought a lot of new things over the years, but every time he did, the same thing happened: He had a few good feelings that were soon swallowed up by a familiar emptiness.

Like a lot of us, Gary was trying to fill his emptiness with what he could buy. But that never works. When we bring things into our lives to try and satisfy an inner need, we eventually discover that what once looked to be so good and satisfying has just added to the clutter with which we've filled our lives. We get more and more things, until one morning we wake up and discover we are still empty. New things have a temporary fulfillment, but before long the old pain creeps back in. Then we find ourselves worse off than before and feeling even more defeated.

As Gary used things to hide his addiction from himself and others, the addiction grew stronger. For awhile he was getting high two or three days a week. Then, before long, he was high every day of the week. He couldn't keep a job, much less get to work on time. Still, he had enough money and support to keep him from living on the streets. He was what is often called a "functioning addict," someone who has a strong addiction yet can keep his life together enough to make it seem like everything is okay. For functioning addicts, life becomes a deception, a constant effort to hide the truth behind a lie.

It's amazing how well some functioning addicts can play that game. I know one man who did it for twenty-two years. Every morning, he would leave his house with a fifth of liquor in his lunch box, and when he came home in the evening, the bottle would be empty. Yet, he still kept his job and paid his bills. As a matter of fact, he drove a tractor trailer every day.

Many functioning addicts are able to hide their addiction because they can hold on to a job and have enough money to keep paying the bills. Money seems to provide an answer for a lot of things. It can shield us from the harsh consequences of our harmful behavior. Money can leave us in bondage with the illusion that we are really free. No, we're not on the street begging or standing in the unemployment line. We may be going about our regular day as if everything is fine, but we have the same problem as any other addict. We have the same need for structure, character, and accountability.

The attraction of the "good life" is not limited to those who have grown up with a lot of money. George, another man in our program, grew up in a very poor neighborhood. But not everyone was poor. He was fascinated by the few people he saw riding around in nice cars, wearing nice clothes, living in nice homes. Things sure seemed to be a lot easier for those people, so naturally, that seemed like a desirable lifestyle. "I thought I was entitled to those things because I didn't have them," he said.

George didn't realize that the people he was

watching had gotten the money to buy those things by dealing drugs. Success—really a wrong idea of what success means—is a trap that catches a lot of people, and George got caught in that trap for many years. He became a drug dealer to try to achieve a certain lifestyle, but he didn't realize all of the other things that lifestyle included—hurting other people, lying, stealing, breaking the law. He knew that selling drugs was wrong, but he tried to justify his behavior by using some of his money to help his mother.

For George, things didn't work out as he had planned. Even the money and the things it bought never gave him the answers he was looking for. In fact, it was just the opposite. As he put it, "Everything I thought was positive turned out to be negative."

Though Gary and George had come from different backgrounds, the result was the same: When they tried to find their satisfaction by acquiring nice things, they were just slipping deeper into bondage. On one level, their lives reflected success. But on the inside—where it counts—they were anything but successful. In fact, their addiction had caused them to lose confidence in themselves, because that new lifestyle went against everything that they knew was right.

Though material things—the things that we can see, touch, smell, taste, and hear—are typically the first to attract our attention, it is the unseen things that have the more powerful effects on our lives and our patterns of behavior. Because of their invisibility, these unseen habits can become so much a part of our lives that we fail to recognize them. But they *will* change us, and if left unchecked, they will become a part of our lives. We take on that new identity of addiction. It's clear then, that if we're going to get free of our addiction, we not only have to recognize these patterns, but we also have to confront them.

What, then, are some of these other, less obvious things that feed our addiction and keep us trapped in a life of bondage? There are many, but let's start with a familiar one.

The Hidden Dragon

Anger is common among people who have an addiction, but it's not always easy to recognize. That's because anger takes on a lot of different forms. Sometimes anger is directed toward other people in loud, aggressive ways like shouting or throwing things. Other times, it appears as a quiet withdrawal or refusal to follow through on basic responsibilities. And then there's the anger that's directed back toward ourselves, the kind that can eventually result in a deep depression that's hard to shake.

You may have seen glimpses of anger in your

own life. Then again, maybe you haven't. Like our addiction, anger is one thing we don't like to talk about or admit. But as long as anger has freedom to roam unchecked in our lives, it will continue to cause destruction.

In our program, we don't deal with anger directly at first. As soon as a man knows that's where I'm headed, he starts putting up walls of defense. All of a sudden he will start being very nice to me, so accommodating, so friendly.

Just because you have a problem with anger doesn't mean you're always showing your anger to other people around you. We can act and move and talk in a way that makes other people think that we're one of the most easy-going people they've ever met.

But our families know better. Probably our closest friends do, too. They've seen the explosions. We may be quick to bottle the anger back up, but it doesn't just disappear. It's often close to the surface, ready to boil out again if we're provoked.

Sometimes—maybe most of the time—we may not hear the anger in our own voices, but others can. "I wasn't angry!" we say. But we were and probably still are. Instead of admitting it, we might say we got a little frustrated or that we were having a discussion. We have even stopped calling it anger. But anger won't go away by being

73

ignored or denied. You can't just walk away from who you are, what has happened to you, or what you have done to other people and expect all of the hurt just to go away. You have to face your past. But, as we will see, you don't have to face it alone.

If you met James, you would probably say that he was a model of kindness. That's what several other men and I thought, too. When I first started walking away from my addiction, James was one of the people in a residential program I was attending. James was always there when you needed him, always encouraging you, always being an example of the right way to live. For 364 days James had been our role model, our leader. When it came time for him to graduate from the program, many of us were there to say good-bye.

The program we were all in at the time had a rule that when you left the property to go home, a family member had to come pick you up. James had wanted his girlfriend to come and get him, but the director told him no.

That's when we saw the real James.

He yelled. He cussed. He wanted to fight. He became so raging mad that he kicked down a small fence.

None of us could believe what we were seeing. It was so unlike the man we had grown to respect and admire over the last year or so.

"Is that James?" we asked each other. "Not James!"

He had hidden himself and his anger so well that no one could see who he really was. He had learned to hide himself from the true issue of living a productive life. He had learned how to cover up the real issues that had hurt him. He had even learned to play the part of a leader and teacher, an example to the rest of us.

Almost every man I know who has an issue with addiction—whether he's come through our program or not—has experienced a great sense of loss. James was no exception. He had seen his father shot. He had been the object of strong racial hatred. He grew up fighting almost every day. His home was poor, with no electricity or running water. If he got one meal a day, he was thankful.

Other men have lost their families, their friends, and everything they've ever owned. They come with nothing but the clothes on their back. These aren't excuses. They're the reality of a lifestyle of addiction.

When we finally realize that we've lost someone or something important to us, it's then that we can become angry, because anger is often part of the process of grieving those losses. Grieving isn't just something we do when a loved one dies; we actually grieve for any deep loss we experience.

For some people who have lived in a lifestyle of addiction, that sense of loss—and the anger they felt about it—began in childhood. They may have experienced the loss of a parent and grown up in a single-parent home, or perhaps they did not know the love of one or both of their parents. They may have lost trust as they suffered abuse or rejection. And they may have lost hope, as their own hopes for change were beaten down again and again through the cycle of poverty or perhaps as a result of their own rebellion.

They've lost more than they can explain or understand. They need to grieve, to pick up again with their lives, to move forward, but they're caught in the cycle of anger. It's fairly common to see people who have allowed the hurt and pain they have experienced to shape their lives, until the anger reaches a point that they just don't know how to deal with it.

Even our natural reactions to pain can become part of the vicious cycle that seems to trap us. Our angry behavior typically produces angry responses that in turn seem to justify our anger. The other day, one of the men in the program explained it something like this: "When I was living in anger, I had to keep being angry. If someone stopped being angry with me, I had to go out and pick a fight with someone else. I always needed an enemy. Otherwise I had no excuse for my behavior."

The structure of our program helps identify the hidden anger in a man's life. As soon as we touch that anger, it's like touching an open sore. By listening to and observing the men, we can often discern the wound he cannot see himself.

But not all anger comes from wounds of loss, abuse, or rejection. Some of the anger we see in ourselves and others comes from a lack of proper discipline or correction.

Chuck came to us with little or nothing. We don't charge for our program, so he wasn't paying us anything. In fact, we were giving him quite a bit. He had a serious dental problem, and we took him back and forth to the dentist and paid for his dental care. Although I didn't realize it at the time, Chuck was expecting us to do this. For the last several years he had expected others to go out of their way to help him, and they had done it. They had continued taking care of him even though this man was thirty-five years old.

After he had been on the property for several months, it came time for him to request a weekend pass. Instead of accepting the usual number of days for the pass, Chuck asked for extra time.

We had gone so far out of our way to help him already—with the dental work and other things—that I was concerned the other men might feel like we were playing favorites if I granted his request for extra time, too. When I told him that, it was obvious I had said something unacceptable.

Finally he said, "Well, I think it's just time for me to leave the program."

"Chuck," I said. "That's hard for me to believe. We have given you more than any of the other men have received. We have stuck by you and supported you. Now, just because I won't give you what you want, you're going to leave?"

He was free to go, so I granted his request. One of the staff members went with him to his room so Chuck could pack up his things. Once in his room, the staff person that had accompanied him began to talk to Chuck about all of our efforts to support him. Chuck started disagreeing with him and, to the staff member's surprise, began kicking and screaming on the floor. It was like watching a five-year-old.

We didn't find out until later that Chuck had already told someone during his weekly phone call that he would be able to get some extra time. He was so sure we would let him have an extra privilege. Hadn't we been doing that all along? Wasn't that what he was used to—getting his way?

Chuck's response is just one example of why we talk about the patterns of a lifestyle of addiction. Chuck came to our program to find a solution for what he thought was a drug problem. But as we looked at his life, it was obvious that he had a rebellion problem: He didn't want to listen or obey. As we found out later, Chuck's mom never corrected him; as a young boy, he always got his way. That was one of the root problems that had continued to feed his addiction.

After Chuck calmed down, the staff member who had accompanied Chuck to his room came back to me and said, "Can we keep him in the program?"

As you can see, the men on my staff have a heart to help people. They know how hard it can be to make it in the battle to overcome life-controlling addictions.

Even though I wasn't sure we could help Chuck, I listened to my staff, and we kept him in the program. I even granted Chuck the extra time he wanted on his pass. I could see that he still didn't understand why I hadn't given it to him in the first place, but we were at a crossroads with Chuck. I had to make a decision whether or not to end our relationship with him then and there, or to extend hope to him one more time. I also knew that he wouldn't believe that I cared about him unless I gave him something. What seemed to be an intense moment allowed me to see the real issue with Chuck.

A couple of days later when he came back from his weekend pass, he was a little embarrassed.

"I acted like a fool," he told me. "I took advantage of you. Yet you still blessed me."

Chuck realized that we had helped him when he didn't deserve it. In the past, he had always thought he deserved to be helped, but now he was seeing something different. We had put our finger on the true addiction. His outburst of anger had brought out his hidden issue of rebellion.

I'm sorry to say that Chuck didn't want to address that issue; it seemed too overwhelming to him. Instead, he chose to withdraw. He became very quiet, just going through the motions of the program. Six months later, when it came time to discuss his progress before he graduated from the first phase of the program, Chuck called a friend to come pick him up. He apparently didn't want to talk about anything. Chuck came into the program "in control" of his life, and he left the program "in control" of his life. He had cleaned off the surface so that the outward appearance looked good, but the inner turmoil—the pattern of behavior that fed his addiction—was basically untouched.

Gifted Without Boundaries

Anger is almost always a negative emotion, but positive things can also serve as snares in our lifestyle of addiction. Like the quiet front we put on to try and hide our anger, we can use our gifts—our natural abilities and inclinations—to hide who we really are.

I know a man who was friends with a prominent national leader, an individual gifted in many ways. In fact, my friend said, he had never met anyone who was more talented. "But," he added, "he was gifted without boundaries."

What did he mean by that? This leader frequently gave in to the whims of his thoughts and desires. He failed to live by sound principles of order and structure, yet because of his position of authority and his natural charm, he usually managed to "smooth things over." His gifts had helped him not only to get by, but also to excel in several areas. He was ambitious and set his sights high. And in the eyes of many he was extraordinarily successful.

Yet just like James, the man in the program I mentioned earlier, this leader was hiding behind his abilities. His gifts spoke so loudly for him that few people could hear the real man inside. If you could hear who he really was, you would probably hear a man who needed help dealing with life-controlling issues that were beginning to surface and affect his reputation.

Eventually, he put himself in a place where he became known for his disgrace as much as for his gifts.

So many of us can fall into this trap, and the only way I know to avoid it is to have the right boundaries of people, places, and things in your life. The boundaries protect the gift in you, and they also protect you. They help hold you accountable, and they give you insight and direction. In time, all of this will produce character, but remember that building character takes time.

Though this prominent leader saw his blessings turned to shame and disgrace, the good news is that it's not over for him. The negative course of his life can be changed and corrected. The challenge he faces is this: Will he be honest enough to admit where he is and be willing to work on the people, places, and things in his life?

James also used his gifts to gain recognition from others. He got married, and he and his wife had two children. He went to seminary, earned his degree, and was ordained in his father-in-law's church. He also oversaw the men's ministry and the deacons' ministry in that church. In time, James became a preacher who spoke to huge crowds of people, often with great effect.

After all his accomplishments, though, James could not hide the deep wounds in his life: the rejection of having to move from one foster home to another; the painful memory of seeing a policeman kill his father; the hurt and anger he had experienced growing up in a segregated and racist community. These things affected his life deeply. Sometimes James would preach, take up a collection, and then use that money to support his addiction. Then, of course, he'd disappear for a couple of months.

Years later, James came to me offering advice about how to run a program for people with addictions. After I listened awhile, I encouraged him to begin working on some of his life-controlling issues.

But it was too hard for him to do by himself. I believed it was my job to help him, but he would have to be willing to work with me. Unless James is able to work on that "inner man," the person he really is on the inside, he will most likely just keep making excuses for himself. And if anyone sees his wounds and seeks to address them, he will attempt to discredit that individual so he won't have to open up that door in his life. He will use his gifts like a weapon to hide his controlling issues: his low self-esteem, anger, deceitfulness, jealousy, and rebellion. These issues have been a part of his life for a long time, but the addiction has just magnified them. That means he will have to work even harder to hide them, but sooner or later he will have to confront those issues because it will be a matter of life or death.

So many gifted men like James have come through our program. I look around and see many potential teachers and leaders. But there has been an opposing force in their lives, and it's created a lot of destruction by encouraging these men to ignore the building blocks of structure, character, and accountability.

It may sound surprising, but I know a lot of men who fall back into addiction every time they start to use their gifts. They may even use words like "calling" or "destiny" to describe what they're doing. But if any of us chooses to live without boundaries, the plans we make to reach our fulfillment will actually lead us to destruction. Instead of the success we hoped for, we will be left with disappointments.

Busy Going Nowhere

Another way we can avoid dealing with our life-controlling problems is by staying busy. When I say "busy," I'm not talking about using your time wisely, being faithfully involved in your family, or having a reasonable job that provides for your needs. We should all be busy in those ways.

But filling up our schedule with too many activities—even good ones—can easily distract us from the real issues of our lives. Take Hank, for example.

For the first month he was in our program, Hank was the picture of a joyful, contented man. He had come from a hard place in his life to a place of peace and rest. He was so positive about everything around him. Then, I noticed that something was changing, in a way that has become familiar. Hank, like many men before him, had reached the point where he needed to deal with some of the deeper issues in his life. I wanted to help prepare Hank for the upcoming battle.

"The celebration is over," I warned him. "The pain in your life is coming out again. You're going to have to take a look at the problems that have brought you to this program."

A few days later, I saw him sitting over in a corner, a deep frown on his face.

I could see that he was in that first phase of dealing with his issues, that place where he had to make a choice: Would he move forward into a new life, or retreat back into the old one?

"You're having to confront some tough issues right now, aren't you?" I asked.

"Yes," he said, "what am I supposed to do?"

"You have to be honest about where your life is today. You have been on a downward spiral. You've destroyed your marriage. You've been a failure as a husband and a father. And you could probably add several more things that I'm not aware of. But most of all, you need to stop blaming others for your lifestyle and behavior. This is the reason you came here. Now is when the work begins."

For Hank, and for every man who comes into our program, this is the time when they can start to make some lasting changes. It starts by taking things one day at a time. It took many years for them to get where they are, and change will not necessarily happen quickly. And it requires commitment. Hank was not quite ready to make any changes, so he did what a lot of others do: He began to focus on everything around him so he wouldn't have to focus on himself. For starters, he began to be critical of just about everyone. In addition, Hank became amazingly busy with all sorts of things—not productive, just busy.

Hank had spent fourteen years in the penitentiary, and there was a lot that scared him when he thought about facing that past and making some genuine changes. Criticism focused the problem on others. Staying busy kept his mind engaged with something else. What he was really trying to do was run, but all he was doing was running in place.

One of the most obvious signs of addiction is avoiding the real issues, the controlling problems that have kept you in bondage. No one wants to look at his life when he has destroyed his marriage, his relationship with his kids, and his finances. I know what Hank was going through. Sometimes I find myself just busy, busy, busy— always on the run. And whom am I running from? I'm running from myself, because I don't want to stand still long enough to take a look at myself, to ask the hard questions about what it will take to see change in yet another area of my life.

I remember the times when I have slowed down long enough to ask those hard questions, and I remember not having the answers. It seems easier to stay busy, to have an excuse not to slow down. Of course, as long as Hank or any of us refuses to slow down, we're going to stay right where we have always been. We're going nowhere as long as we are running in place.

How do we slow down? It's not easy. There are plenty of excuses, and we have used those excuses so often, they seem like the truth. But each of us needs to stop and take a good look at ourselves. Otherwise, we will never identify the things that have kept us in defeat, and sooner or later, we'll find out that we have been defeated again.

Under Control?

In one sense, every man who struggles with a life-controlling issue such as a drug addiction also struggles with his own "need" to control his life. It makes sense when you think about it. When our lives are out of control, we seek stability in some area so we don't have to focus on the real issues.

The men we've looked at in this chapter used a lot of different things to present the image that they were still in control, that there were no serious issues in their lives. Whether it was having a lot of nice things, presenting the image of a successful preacher, or just staying busy, each wanted to hide the emptiness inside. But things, appearances, and activities will not fill up that empty place. As one of the men in our program put it, "You can do all the right things and still be torn up on the inside."

Maybe this is a picture of where some of us are today. We look successful and stay busy, but if we're honest enough to admit it, we're still wounded. We've got a deep issue that's created a lot of destruction. We may be able to hide our anger, at least with most people, because it only comes to the surface every now and then. When morning comes, we get up, get dressed for work, and pretend that everything is under control.

Some people can keep living like this for a long time. Yet, the longer we keep up the appearance, the worse things become. Everything seems fine, but inside the pain is growing. We won't just stay where we are. We'll keep getting lower, and there is no bottom to this pit.

Once we get to this level, we're only concerned with numbing the pain inside. Some of us may take on financial obligations that we cannot afford. Some may turn to a new relationship that seems to offer comfort for the moment, but it requires a commitment we cannot keep. And some of us will turn to drugs or alcohol. Even though we understand what the drugs will do to us, we're desperate for something to fill up that emptiness, something to distract us from the pain.

So we pursue the drug over and over again. Before we know it, before we really understand what is happening, the drug addiction is out of control, and we become helpless and hopeless. Now we can't hide any longer. It's not just that we can't hide the addiction, but we can't hide *ourselves* either. The greed, the lust, and the anger all come to the surface. We may lose everything that is precious to us—our family, our friendships, our possessions. But the addiction isn't to blame. All the addiction does is reveal what's really going on inside.

At this point, a lot of people will focus on the addiction as the main problem. It seems to make sense. Our life was under control *before* we started using drugs, we tell ourselves. But it never was.

Even if we do focus on the addiction and are able to "stop it" for a while, the addiction will probably return. What we really need to do is go back and address the anger, the lust, the hatred, the emptiness. Only then can we break the addiction.

The point is that even our best efforts at control are only cover-ups. Some people are better at it than others, but they're only playing a game, a game they are sure to lose.

The Next Step

If you've been honest with yourself up to this

point, you're probably aware of some of the people, places, and things that have been fueling your addiction. You may be discouraged, even overwhelmed. That's natural, and you're not alone.

I began by saying something that I want you to remember: If there was a way into this, there's got to be a way out.

As you look at your own life, you will likely find a number of things that you associate with your lifestyle of addiction. But there will always be more than you can see by yourself. And seeing those things is only the first step.

How will you be successful in this process? Only by taking one step at a time. If you look at everyone else around you, you'll find that no one ever does more than that. That's all I ever did, and, believe me, I found a lot of grace along the way. The same can be true for you, too. All you have to do to begin is put one foot in front of the other.

THE BENEFITS
OF PEOPLE, PLACES & THINGS

CHAPTER FIVE:

People You Need

One of my first jobs after I began living a drug-free life was at an auto-body shop. The owner, a man who became not only my friend but also my mentor, later told me a secret about how he managed his employees.

"For the first six months," he said, "I don't pay much attention to the way a man works and acts. During that time, he will just try to impress me.

"After six months, he has become familiar with the job and with his coworkers, and I will begin to really see what kind of worker he is."

It's true that most of us are able to sustain hard work for a certain period of time. But after the newness of a situation has worn off, as the work starts getting tough, when we're bored of the same old thing, that's when our true character emerges.

We notice the same thing with the men in our program. Just like Hank (the man I told you about in the last chapter), for the first month in particular, they are so thankful to be there. They are trying to do anything and everything they can to please the staff.

But after a while reality kicks in. This program is going to require them to change, to build character. Just like a good athletic training program, it's going to be tough. They're going to have to stretch themselves into some new areas that will be uncomfortable, and they're going to need to be pushed and encouraged to go further than they thought possible.

What they need to stay with this training program and overcome their addictions are good "coaches," faithful friends who will stand by them. But first they need to give these friends permission to ask the hard questions, to speak the truth.

It's not going to be easy at first; it wasn't for me anyway. It took me quite a few years to learn how to trust. I had to let people into my life slowly. For me, the process turned out to be a double lesson. The people I had most distrusted in my life were white people, and they were the ones who first began reaching out to help me grow and stand on my own two feet.

The challenge we face in learning to trust is this: Trust is based on the truth. Those of us who have struggled with life-controlling issues have spent a lot of our lives not being honest with ourselves and others about our addiction. As a result, our relationships with our families and friends have been based on lies and manipulation. We've said what was convenient, not what was truthful. We've done what we felt like doing, not what we said we would do. People have learned not to trust us, and we haven't trusted them. That's why we've probably had so many broken relationships. We may have had friends just walk out on us, and we didn't understand why. Our marriages may have grown dull and lifeless. We may wonder why we don't have great relationships with our children. And in all of these relationships that have turned "sour" on us, we probably have placed the blame on everyone but ourselves. But if we can open up our lives just a little and be honest with at least one other person, we can change that pattern.

When we tell the truth, we allow others to begin to see us. This gives them an opportunity to correct us, to challenge us, and to encourage us. In short, this new relationship of trust allows the healing to begin in our lives. When we begin to trust, we are taking a step in a completely different direction.

For me, the act of trusting felt as if I was step-ping off a cliff. And in a way, I was. I had never walked this way before, and I wasn't sure that I wanted to. Still, I knew that if I didn't learn to trust, I would return to the bondage that had left me defeated and without hope. I didn't want to go back there, so I took my first step.

As I said, it took time for trust to grow in my life. We have to learn to be patient, because others will make mistakes, and so will we.

Let me warn you about a couple of pitfalls I faced along the way.

False Trust

In the beginning of our walk out of an addictive lifestyle, even though we have determined to trust others, it's easy to fall back into old patterns of lies and deceit. As a result, we can easily wind up convincing ourselves that we are trusting other people, when we really are not.

I have found at least two dangerous substitutes for trust. One is expressed with our words, the other with our actions, but neither is real trust.

The first substitute for trust is saying that we trust—using all the right words—but all the while holding back. We tell ourselves and others that we are letting go of our suspicion and control, but we are really watching people from a distance.

We see this a lot in the men who come into our program. Most of them have little experience of real trust. They may have lived with a parent who was an alcoholic or abusive. Lifestyle choices may have led them to be around people who lied to get their way. Since then, all of their relationships have been weakened, because they have never known the trust that is the beginning of any real relationship. So I tell them, "You're going to have to learn how to trust me."

The majority of these men definitely do want to trust me. They want a way out of their addictive lifestyle. They even tell me they have good reasons to trust me: They have seen how our program has helped others, how my life has been changed, and how I have helped so many men. It's no surprise that their almost immediate response is, "I don't have any other choice but to trust you. You have proven yourself."

But what they are really saying is, "If I were to trust anyone, it would certainly make sense to trust someone like you."

They know about trust, and it sounds like a good idea. But trust isn't an idea; it's an action. Because these men have never experienced trust in their own lives, they have no understanding of what it involves.

Early on in my walk out of a lifestyle of addiction, there was a group of people I needed to trust, and I told myself that I would trust them. But what I was really doing was setting them up for failure. I couldn't make them fail, but I had already decided that it wasn't going to work out, that they would fail me. Why? Because trust hadn't worked with my father, my family, or my other friends who had betrayed me. *Surely,* I said to myself, *these people will fail me, too.*

So I kept them at a distance. My first observations seemed to confirm that I had done the right thing, because from my point of view they began attacking me. They really weren't attacking me, I realized later; they were simply challenging me. They were seeking to put boundaries around my life, to bring structure and order to what I was trying to accomplish. They began to chip away at some ideas I had, and it felt very personal.

Some of the things your friends will address in your life will probably feel like personal attacks, too. You have a vision for your life as a productive individual, but it needs structure and order, just as mine did. You may want to hang out with old friends, start a new relationship, change jobs, or move, but is that really the best choice you can make right now?

The test for trust begins when other people begin saying things we don't want to hear, when they challenge our beliefs and ideas about what is best for us. Then, to stop trusting them seems the best choice. But if we're honest with ourselves, we can look back and see how holding on to our own beliefs and ideas about what is best has gotten us into trouble over and over again. We've blamed others, but we have made the decisions that have kept us defeated. We've been stubborn. We haven't listened because we haven't wanted to change. And not changing those patterns of an addictive lifestyle is what has kept us in bondage.

It's important to trust other people and listen to what they have to say. That doesn't mean we will always get the right answers from them, or that they won't disappoint us. All of us—whether we come from homes disrupted by an addictive lifestyle or not—have experienced broken trust. People are not going to be perfectly trustworthy, but we cannot use that as an excuse to hold onto our old patterns of deceit and distrust.

I mentioned that there are two forms of "false trust" that we are likely to fall into as we walk out of an addictive lifestyle. The first is saying that we trust without really meaning it. But there is a second form of "false trust" that is perhaps more deceptive, and that is when we set up people around us to get our own way.

One of our former students used his family in that way. He convinced them that if he could only get a good apartment, a car, and a job, then things would be fine with him. And his family made sacrifices to provide these things. Yet, because he had not dealt with the underlying life-controlling issues, all of their support was not going to change the obvious problem of his addiction. At the end of it all, he was back in the same place where he had started. Now, not only is this bottomless pit a part of his life, it's becoming a part of theirs as well.

In chapter two, we talked about the ways people in our lives have been part of the problem. One thing we noted about those people was that they were a lot like us, because we naturally gravitate toward people who fit in with our lifestyle. They become a tool that we can use to stay in our addiction, either by enabling us, like the family above, or in some other way.

When we begin taking our first few steps out of an addictive lifestyle, we will be tempted to seek out people just like ourselves, people who won't ask the hard questions. But we won't grow that way. If we choose to be around people who will always agree with us, we just repeat our mistakes. Instead, we need to seek out people who are different. The real friends we need in our lives will want to understand our addiction and the underlying patterns that have been a part of it. They will not be afraid to disagree with us, and they will be willing to challenge us.

That's going to be tough, but I've seen my relationships with people who are different from me work wonders in my life. Just let me warn you about something: They won't be perfect. They will have issues in their own lives, but the things they struggle with will probably be different from the issues you have. They will let you down, too, but it doesn't mean you made a mistake in trusting them, because these are the people who will support you as you find a way out of your old life of brokenness and into a new life filled with opportunities.

So where do we go to find people we can trust? How can we at least help guard ourselves from trusting the wrong kinds of people again? The answers I have to those questions come with a few surprises.

Finding Support

One place to find support might be right in your own community. Seek out someone who once lived a lifestyle of addiction but who has now been "clean" or sober for at least two to three years.

I wouldn't seek a lot of advice from someone who has only been living productively for a year or so. In most cases, they're still dealing with the addiction itself. A lot of the addictive behavior patterns are probably still active in their lives, so they can't help you face and overcome your own behavior patterns.

But if they have been making some real changes, if they are staying free from drugs and alcohol, and if they are establishing some new patterns of thinking and living, these same people can be a huge encouragement. They will give you courage to take a look at yourself. And they will give you hope just by seeing their first successful steps.

Remember, when you're looking for people who have been successful in coming out of an addictive lifestyle, you can't just measure their success by how long they've been sober or free from drugs. Why not? I've seen someone who has been sober for twenty years and still struggles with the addiction, because he's never dealt with the attitudes and behaviors that have fed the addiction. That's why when you're looking for a friend you can trust, you probably won't be making your best choice if you only consider the length of their sobriety.

But former addicts are not the only people who can offer the benefit of their experience and wisdom. In fact, some of the people who helped me the most had never used drugs at all. Yet they knew how to live with order and structure in their lives. They knew how to forgive. They knew how to look beyond the present situation and see future possibilities. And they knew how to hold out hope before me, while still holding me accountable for my life in the here and now.

If you can find people like that, you've found a gold mine.

A Word to Friends and Family

Let me offer a word of caution to those who have tried to support friends or family members who are caught up in a lifestyle of addiction. You may be caught up in the cycle of addiction, too. I don't mean that you've necessarily been involved in drugs or have been drinking to excess. You can be part of the addictive lifestyle without ever having touched alcohol or drugs.

There are many ways the addiction can be at work in your life. You may have tried to protect your friend or spouse, your parent or child, making excuses for them when you knew they were not being honest, or covering up for them when you knew they were doing wrong. Perhaps you refused to hold them accountable, enabling their addiction by tolerating their behavior. You may have tried to control them by hiding or throwing away the objects of their addiction. Whatever it was that you were doing probably wasn't working. Even if you were able to stage a planned confrontation and get the person into a treatment program, you may have been disappointed in the long run.

To break free from those old patterns, you will need to become part of the process of healing, particularly when it comes to learning to trust. Trust is a two-way street, and especially at first, you may need a counselor, someone who can hear both sides and help you work out some positive solutions.

Help begins with being honest. You probably don't understand all of what's been going on or know how to fix it, and that's okay. What you do know is that your friend or family member has not been living the way he's supposed to be living. In the past you may have been reluctant to say anything about it, and you may have made excuses for your silence: *I'm not perfect. Everyone has problems. I'm not a counselor.* We make excuses so we don't have to be accountable, or because we don't feel like we have the right or the wisdom to speak into their lives. But we need to be accountable to each other. We can speak the things that we have observed for the last several years, and we don't need a degree in counseling to do it. We need each other. Be a part of the solution. Remember, it starts with being honest.

There's another danger that friends and family members can easily find themselves in. Once they see change happening in their loved ones, they may try to push that change through to its completion. But some wounds take a long time to heal. You will have to be patient, too. You will want to see certain things happen quickly, but if they happen too quickly, without a proper foundation being laid, it will be far worse in the long run. For example, being promoted too quickly at work can place a man in a dangerous position if he is only recently on the road out of addiction and not yet ready for the responsibility.

I understand that you want your son or your husband back, but he may not come back in the way you remember him. His life has been changed by the addiction, and you will have to change, too, to help him stay free. He needs to protect himself now from things that he didn't used to have to protect himself from before. Just as he needs to see his weakness and his deceit, you also need to see them. Even though your loved one is not engaging in the object of his addiction, don't start thinking that now "everything will be like it always was." You may get pieces of his "old self" back, but now there's a different person in there. Grieve over that loss, but don't stay there. Move forward together so that you can see lasting change.

Also, help him understand, as best you can, the importance of keeping the commitments he has made to himself and his community. This is what will help keep him focused, from going back to his past life. It will remind him of the things over which he has victory. It will also remind him of the lines he cannot cross, of the friends he cannot be around. Keeping his commitments each and every day is one of the most positive things he can do, and you can be a big encouragement along the way.

Steps Toward Trust

Families can be part of the addictive patterns in our own lives, but they can also be the ones who love us more than anyone else. So they can become our strongest support on the other side of addiction.

Over time, I received a lot of love and trust from friends and family. And that changed me. As I received that support, I began to deal with the pain and bondage within—very carefully I began to share about my hurt, pain, and rejection. I also shared about my rebellion and why my heart was so entangled by it. Love softened me again. It allowed me to be honest about my true feelings. I had hardened my heart to the pain a long time ago, but the love of others began to soften my heart again. Eventually, I was able to give out what I had received. In other words, one reason that I can give a lot of love and patience today is because I have received a lot of love and patience.

When I began working with the men in our program, I discovered that their lives became a mirror for my own. I would talk to them about how there was freedom for them in this or that area of their lives, and then I would go home and realize that I was dealing with a lot of the same issues and challenges. As I reached out and started helping them with their issues, I more clearly saw the life-controlling issues I was struggling with.

I had been blaming myself—my rebellion and my disobedience—for my addiction. But as I listened to these men, I began to see how the abuse I received from my father had left me with so much anger and bitterness. I had never considered how being expected to be the man of the house at age ten, or being shot by my father when I was fourteen, had shaped my life. Serving these men opened up a whole new awareness in me, allowing even more healing into my life.

I learned to be more open with my wife and my children. And as I began to be real with them and address the issues in my life that had caused them pain, I found forgiveness there, and much grace. Even today, after seventeen years, I am still learning how to be open about the deeper issues in my life and admit my weaknesses to them. This is an ongoing process of change for me—as it will be for you—but it has to start somewhere.

Friends Without Answers

There's an old story about four men with a good friend who was paralyzed. I imagine they all felt pretty helpless to do anything about it, but they didn't give up and they didn't back away from their friendship.

One day they heard that there was someone in town who had helped a lot of other people with their physical problems. In fact, he was so famous and such great crowds followed him that it was hard to get near him. But the paralyzed man's friends were convinced that this could be the answer for their friend, and they were determined to get him to this man one way or another. So they picked up their paralyzed friend on his mat and started off.

It wasn't hard to follow the crowds, but when they arrived at the house where the famous man was visiting, they were unable to get in the door past the large gathering of people. Without wasting time, they climbed up on the top of the house and began to open a hole large enough to lower their friend through the roof, down to where the man was standing.

As you can imagine, it caused quite a scene. But their efforts were successful, thanks in part to the fact that they would not give up when they didn't have the answer themselves. Because of their faithful persistence, and the faith of their paralyzed friend, they all saw a healing that day that left them amazed.

Sometimes people block the process of friendship and trust by telling themselves that no one will have the answers. "You don't understand what I've been through," they say. I may not, but we can look for an answer together.

Friends shouldn't walk away simply because they don't have all the answers. To be a friend is to trust the relationship that has been built within each other, and honor that when times get hard. A friend who is now my pastor said something important that has blessed the friendship we have today. I walked through his door with something heavy on my heart, something that he could see was challenging my life. As I shared these things with him, he said, "William, I do not have the answer for you. But what I do have, what I can offer you, is that I'm your friend. Whatever it takes, I'm here for you."

He gave me something that I needed much more than an answer; he gave me his friendship. In dealing with people who have an addiction, that same opportunity will come in many different ways—not because we have the answer, but because we are accountable to each other. Accountability allows us to grow, not only with each other, but also within ourselves. Honesty and openness allows us to see more clearly the things that have held us in bondage. And from that point, we can learn how we might overcome them and become truly free.

My pastor didn't give me an answer that day; he gave himself. And a friend was what I needed, someone who would not judge me, someone who would listen.

Remember: True friends are accountable to each other.

The Secret of Submission

At the start of this book, I mentioned that people with addictions often exhibit what seems like an overdeveloped sense of self-confidence. In reality, they have very little confidence. What they have is self-reliance, and they rely on what works for the moment. In other words, they rush from one issue to the next trying to maintain and save what they have. At times they look heroic in this role; at other times they just look tired.

Our self-reliance has worn us down over the years, so maybe it's time to try something else. I've discovered that one answer is submission.

When some of us hear the word *submission*, we think that it's something harsh, a position where someone else has uncontrolled authority over our lives. But that's not what submission is at all. It is really an act of humility and service. That's why there is strength in submission. It helps to reveal our prideful ways and rebellion.

Submission is the key to finding freedom in many areas of our lives. When we submit, we refuse to give ourselves permission to act in any way we want to, to burst out in anger or self-righteousness when things don't go our way. There is freedom in submission as we learn to be obedient. This is totally the opposite of what we have been led to believe.

Submission can begin by being open to someone

else's advice. It is one of the keys to the kind of friendship we have just been talking about. My friend submitted himself to me just by being there for me. He submitted his time and his energy for my benefit. And I was greatly comforted as a friend because of his actions. There have also been times when he has had to reveal to me some of my own life-controlling issues. But because of the friendship he has shown—the love, honesty, and support we have built in each other's lives—it was not as hard for me to submit and listen to his advice.

Here's some wisdom that I heard a long time ago: "The greatest of all must be the servant of all." There is a lot of treasure in those few words. Service and submission are the examples we need as we seek to be responsible for all that we have been given.

Connected with Others

Our addictive patterns were self-centered and irresponsible. Our new life needs to be connected with other people in positive ways as we learn how to live responsibly. Rebellion and selfish independence will defeat us every time. Now is the time to have an ear to listen, a heart to receive, and an openness to put into practice what we hear. For some of us, that will be the key to getting free from our addictive behavior.

Part of this journey is learning how to be connected with others in positive ways. But there is a potential trap even here. Being connected with others and learning to trust them doesn't mean that we become completely dependent on them. If you're looking for people to fight your battles for you or tell you what to do every step of the way, you're not learning to trust; you've just transferred your addiction from one thing to another.

It's important to understand that because of the addictive behavior in our lives, we have a tendency to transfer our addiction to other areas. That dependency can even be transferred to the positive things we have set up in our lives to help us stay free of our addiction and the patterns that have fueled it. In other words, as adults, we can become so overly dependent on friends and relatives that we develop the attitude that they are there to take care of us. That's an unhealthy relationship. That's a piece of the addictive behavior that has to be overcome.

Friends are there to support us and to encourage us, to walk beside us. But our battles are there for *us* to fight. We don't fight them alone, but no one can fight them for us while we watch from a distance. The challenges are part of the process of our healing. Our friends and family can help point out our addictive behavior, but we have to acknowledge it and work to change it. Unless we face our current battle, we will miss crucial areas of character building and growth that will prepare us for the next battle we will face.

In my life, I look at the bridges behind me to give me strength to cross the bridge before me. When I faced the challenges from my own extended family, I didn't have the answers. So I looked back and remembered. I remembered the victory I had seen when I first came out of the drug world, when I was still living in a neighborhood that was infected with that lifestyle. I went back to when I had nothing and yet still had everything, because I had hope and faith that one day, as I put these basic principles into practice, I would find the freedom I longed for. I had seen the faithfulness of a strength greater than my own. Our family had not only survived, we had prospered there. Even though I was making barely enough money to get by, there was always enough—always a car of some sort to drive to work, always time to help a neighbor, and always something to give to those who needed a helping hand.

One of the biggest challenges in learning to trust are the people who will deliberately take advantage of us. It's sad to say, but we can find them without looking very far. Still, we can't let them become our excuse for closing off our relationships with other people and refusing to deal with the hurt in our lives. One of my definitions of trust is allowing a friend to speak into areas of our lives that are uncomfortable, areas that are hard to change.

When we come across people who break our trust, whether they do it deliberately or not, it's time to buckle down and say, "I know this isn't going to be easy, but I'm going to leave the door of trust open in my life until I find someone who can grow with me in learning how to trust. If I close that door, it's going to be ten times worse than what I'm going through now, because I'll be right back in bondage again."

The broken trust we have experienced in the past can create fear in our lives. We become sensitive to people breaking their trust with us again. Wise counsel can help us work through this. Don't let the people who have let you down take you off the path of walking free from your addiction. Yes, it can be challenging, but it is part of the process. Trust will allow healing to continue to happen in your life. It will take time, but you'll see, and you'll be amazed at the change that can occur. I've seen it happen in my own life and in the lives of a lot of others.

Learn to have faith in the process. In other words, understand that as you take each new step, you're getting closer to your final goal. For me, I had to also learn to have faith in a strength beyond my own. My friends or my family weren't enough, and as I said before, my own strength wasn't enough. I started to open my life up slowly to a spiritual reality. And as I did so, it gave me the strength to face my past.

I truly believe that in order for you to walk in freedom, you have to have an openness to walk in a spiritual reality and a life of faith. For me, that faith and trust has helped me learn to trust others a little more each day.

THE BENEFITS
OF PEOPLE, PLACES & THINGS

CHAPTER SIX:

Places of the Heart

As we talked about in the first part of this book, once our heads and bodies have been free from drugs or alcohol for a little while, after we've gotten a new job, maybe even some new friends—when life is looking good—it's sometimes easy to think that everything has changed, including our old ways of thinking. But we should be careful before making a quick decision about that.

Let me give you an example of what I'm talking about.

One of the guys from our program, Fred, had just graduated when he joined a support group. Those in the group knew something about his past and his struggle with crack cocaine. They were encouraging in many ways, but they didn't understand completely about Fred's addiction and the thought patterns that had helped to fuel it. So they took him to a bar.

When I discovered what had happened, I

confronted Fred. You might be able to guess what he said in response:

"But I wasn't drinking."

Sometimes a place that seems to look different is really the same old place in disguise. To Fred, the bar may not have seemed so bad. He was with men who cared about him, who wanted to support him in his desire to be drug-free. Fred had convinced himself that there was nothing wrong with going into a bar.

"I've got a crack problem," he told me.

"But both alcohol and the environment you're in can trigger that," I reminded him.

Fred was confident he knew best. "I can drink a beer," he insisted.

"No," I told him, "you can't drink a beer. You've been in bondage for ten years, and if you don't know you can't drink a beer, then you don't understand your addiction."

So he went to the bar again, believing that it was okay for him to have a drink. Two days later he was back on crack cocaine. Four months later he was stealing, completely back into his old way of living, his old mindset. And it had all started when he thought he could go into that bar.

It's not uncommon after someone has been off a drug for a while—when they begin to feel better and the memory of the pain is fading a little—that they believe they have conquered the problem. Or maybe they begin to think that there was no problem in the first place. Then, even those obviously wrong places may become some of the first places they go back to. If there's "no problem," then why not?

If you convince yourself that you have never had a problem with alcohol, or that you're now in control of your addiction, you may have also convinced yourself that there's nothing wrong with going to a bar or even bringing a six-pack back to your house so you can "relax" every now and then. I tell you, that's a dangerous place to go in your mind. Thinking that way doesn't prove that you've gotten rid of the addiction. All it proves is that you have learned to function in your addiction.

Fred had crossed a line into a place where he didn't have the strength to stand. Being in the bar and drinking that beer planted some seeds in his mind. His choice also revealed a weakness in his character: He thought he was still in control, that he could flirt on the edge of danger and walk away unharmed.

In fact, there was a deeper problem than the addiction, and that was rebellion. Fred had made up his mind to do what he wanted to do. From what I understand, he had been that way for a big part of his life, and now his rebellion was helping him walk back into a place of defeat.

It's so easy to put ourselves in the same places where we have experienced defeat in the past and now, somehow, expect different results this time around. We say, "This is different. This is not the same girlfriend I had before," or, "I'm at this party with a whole new group of friends."

We're only deceiving ourselves.

There are some places you simply need to stay away from, whether you are engaging in the object of your addiction or not. Those places will differ with every person reading this book, but as we mentioned in chapter three, they are the places that can trigger our addictions. They are danger zones for us, no matter how familiar, safe, or even fun they may seem.

What we need to remember is that it's not the appearance we present, or even the length of time we've been sober that matters. It's what goes on inside of us—those hidden patterns—that will eventually tell the story of what is going to happen next. Let me give you an example.

I remember going to a meeting once where there were several drug and alcohol addicts trying to support each other to stay away from their addiction. As part of admitting his problem, one man went into great detail about his last drug experience. He talked about what drug he used, how he prepared the drug, how it felt to get high, and on and on.

He gave such vivid details, that listening to him was almost like being there and sharing his experience. Afterward, my focus wasn't on staying away from my addiction, but on getting back to it. There I was in a meeting that was supposed to help me find relief from my craving and desires, but what I was hearing just made those desires stronger. All I could think of was, "When is this meeting going to be over so I can go out and get high, too?"

Evidently, I was not the only person who was thinking this way. When the day for the next meeting rolled around, several of the guys didn't show up. I'm sad to say that they were back in the rehabilitation center after having had a setback.

Don't get me wrong. I believe that these types of meetings can offer a lot of support, especially when someone is just beginning to move away from their addiction. Again, the point I'm making is that even an apparently safe place can hold dangers for us if we're not aware of them.

Beyond the negative places we need to avoid, what are the positive places we need to go? Where are they, and how do we get there? That's basic information we're going to need.

Staying Focused

I frequently see some of the men in our program get restless. We ask them to make an initial eighteen-month commitment to learn how to live a productive life. That's a year and a half living away from friends and family, away from a regular job, away from all of their usual activities. And while they are with us, they are being challenged to look at the basic assumptions and patterns of their lives in ways they've never had to before.

It's not an easy place to be. Often, after two or three months, some of them say, "My time here is finished. I've got to leave and get on with my life." These are men who have child support and restitution to pay, who have families to care for. All of these sound like good reasons to leave, but that man has to get his own life straight first to be able to help support others.

Though he doesn't see it now, all of those needs—the ones that he thinks are giving him a good excuse to leave—are really just detours, distractions that will lead him in the wrong direction. Unless he stays on the path straight before him, he will end up back in the same old place of defeat and bondage, and he will most likely be amazed at finding himself there again.

Since we have a voluntary program, no one can be forced to stay against their will, so every now and then a man will decide he's ready to leave. He'll pack up his things, ask someone to pick him up, and move on with his life. A few days later, reality sets in: "By the way, where am I going?" In other words, he will be thinking, *Where will I live? Where will I work? How will I pay child support and restitution? What lie or excuse can I make up to convince my family to accept me back into their life, their home, and their finances?*

Some of these men leave and never come back. Others, after they realize they rushed off too soon, return and begin the process again.

Jeff came into our program struggling to have his own way. He wanted to get rid of his drug addiction, but he also wanted to hold on to his old lifestyle, and that included his anger and self-reliance. Eventually he decided he didn't want to be in the program any longer, so he went back home to his family. Eventually, he realized that the things we had been trying to teach him were true, because he no longer had control of his life and his behavior.

Three months later, he called and asked to come back into the program. Of course, we said yes. When Jeff arrived, he had a new attitude and openness. He began putting the things he was learning into practice in his own life. In time, he became one of our responsible student leaders and eventually graduated.

Today Jeff has a successful job working with highly technical equipment in the career of his choice. He had always known he had potential. But his earlier pursuit of career and college education had distracted him from dealing with the behavior of his addiction. What Jeff needed was some time to focus on the wounds in his life that kept robbing him of his potential. Because he came back to us the second time with the right focus, he is now able to use his gifts to benefit both himself and others.

You, too, are going to have to stay on track in order to be successful. There will be a lot of detours—opportunities to move on with your life—that look reasonable, even necessary. But some of those detours are distractions that can lead you back into a place of defeat. Just like Jeff, you may find that your focus on these distractions will blind you to the truth of your addictive behavior, the patterns in your life that have been robbing you of success.

Let me give you another example of what I'm talking about.

A Good Opportunity

Jim was known for the good work he did. In fact, while Jim was in our program, his employer phoned me to say that Jim could have his old job back after he finished our program, if he wanted it. The people at his old job really cared about him, and I could tell they had Jim's best interests at heart.

After he graduated, Jim did go back to work for that company, and it seemed he had an important part of his life in place. Not long after he started back to work, however, I happened to run into him. He told me that he had been offered another job: better pay, more benefits, and so on.

To most people, that sounds like a good opportunity, but for Jim it wasn't. Jim hadn't learned to be faithful to those who had been faithful to him. He hadn't learned that in order to grow, he not only needs to walk through the process, but he also needs to learn patience and contentment. The increased benefits and pay that Jim got in his new job would have eventually been offered in his old job where the people cared about him. Their small company was more like family than a workplace. There was no limitation there because those people had a love and respect for Jim, and whenever there is love and respect there is always opportunity.

But Jim was focused on something else. He had restitution to pay and child support; he had four children and was getting ready to get married. In a very short time since leaving our program, he had put too much financial responsibility on himself. Obviously, he was looking for a way to make more money. But he was now so focused on his immediate need that he had lost sight of the more important things.

Jim was at a crossroad, and he had a decision to make. Was he going to stay at his job and build character and accountability, something he had never been willing to do before? Or was he going to go back to his old way of doing things his own way?

I told him, "Jim, don't give up a good opportunity where you are now, for a quick fix somewhere else." But he wasn't listening. He made the same decision he had always made: to go his own way. He took the new job and his pay increase of just one dollar an hour!

In a fairly short time that new job ended, and Jim found himself back in the same place he was before. He also got in trouble with the law, not only because he couldn't pay his child support or his restitution, but also because he was facing a drug charge. No longer did he have the opportunity to be a father or a husband, things he had told me over and over again were so significant to him.

For men who come from an addictive lifestyle, it's so important to be faithful to our commitments. It all goes back to contentment. When we're content, we are able to move slowly enough to benefit from the process.

You may realize you've wasted years of your life, and you're in a hurry to get where you think you should be now. Where is that?—Working in a new job? Driving a nicer car? Getting all your bills paid off? Moving to a better neighborhood? Getting married?

I want to encourage you to take a look at where you are now. Like Jim, are you in a good job where people respect you and want to help you and stand by you? Do they know you, know about your past, and still accept you for who you are? If so, that job offers you a lot more than a steady paycheck.

Don't let your restlessness cause you to overlook the building blocks necessary for your foundation. Don't make decisions that might look good now, but after a period of time may put you back in a place of danger in terms of your addiction.

Work It Through

You may find that you're tempted to leave your current job or another situation because of some challenges you're facing. Maybe you're finding it difficult to get along with certain people. Unless you have contentment when things are not working out as you expected, you're going to look for a detour, one that will probably take you right back to where you were. You'll justify it. You might convince yourself that you have to provide for yourself, even if it means breaking the law. You might even make some money and pay off some of those bills. But when it's all said and done, you'll find yourself in the same old place of bondage, just like Jim—no better off than when you started.

I guarantee that for each and every person who goes back to his old ways because he lacks contentment, there is a way out if he stays the course. The road may seem a little rocky or even look as if it's blocked, but if he refuses to turn back, he will find a way—an opportunity—ahead of him. Contentment will help keep him focused on the right path.

Some of us who struggle with a lifestyle of addiction have a tendency to make spontaneous decisions, without really thinking things through clearly. Unless we have a clear direction, we shouldn't start off in just any direction. It's often better to wait instead of letting our situation or circumstances "push" our lives in a wrong direction. Choosing our own way can sometimes be one of the biggest mistakes we can make.

Finishing Up

One of the old patterns in your life may have been not finishing one thing before starting another. That tendency can show up in any area of your life. That's the way it was with Doug.

Doug was gifted in several areas, and while he was in our program, he put those gifts to use in a new business venture we were starting. The business was a way for the men to learn new skills as well as a means to help our entire program become more financially self-sufficient. Doug helped a great deal in getting our new business underway, but he had some unfinished business in his own life that soon began showing up in his work.

For years Doug had been used to getting his way. I knew that he had walked out on countless jobs and opportunities in the name of "I-couldn't-get-what-I-wanted." I could see the process happening all over again. There were five projects in the shop in various stages of being finished, and Doug was asking for a brand-new project to start.

The men got a little fed up with him because Doug was trying to stay in control of everything. He was micromanaging them, looking for faults. He cared more about his success than he cared about developing others' gifts and skills, and he often spoke to his colleagues harshly.

Whenever they tried to approach him with a word of correction, Doug would say, "Well, why don't we just close the shop down?" I told him that they weren't attacking the shop; they were addressing his character. His management of the shop was so bad that the men didn't even want to work with him. But he never seemed to understand. What Doug was really saying was, "I can tell you what to do, but don't point out any weakness in my life."

Eventually, Doug decided he was going to leave the program. Just because we hadn't done what he wanted us to do, he was going to leave us with those unfinished projects, as he had done with other people so many times before. He knew that we were trying to become more financially self-sufficient, and he believed that there was no one else at that time who could do what he was doing. So his way of getting what he wanted was to bail out. It wasn't until I stood up to that childish part of him that something positive began to happen.

If Doug wanted to go, I was going to let him go. I had plenty of experience doing most of the things he was doing for us. I let him know that. When he saw that I could get the work done without him, he changed his mind and decided he wanted to stay after all. He realized that he wasn't indispensable, that we could get along without him.

He returned to the projects with a completely different attitude. The other men got along with him for the most part, and he began to teach the men some of the skills he had learned. I wish I could tell you that he kept doing that, but he didn't. And there came a time when Doug finally had to be dismissed.

Today, Doug is a prime example of a man whose life is completely out of control but who still won't let go of the things holding him back. He's gone back to living a life of lying, stealing, and drugs. His behavior of addiction has brought death to his gifts and talents, to his relationships, and to the opportunities that his friends have offered him. And, even though he may not see it, that same behavior has the potential to bring physical death to him as well.

For most of his life, Doug has been like a mountain climber who ventures halfway up the mountain and then stops. He started out to reach the shelter on the mountain top, but for some reason he didn't keep going. Maybe he became satisfied with his progress, or maybe he was just too afraid to take the next step. But he cannot stop on the side of the mountain and call it home. Nor can we. We've got to get to the top of the mountain. That's where our safety is. We can't just pick and choose the areas we want to work on in our lives and then stop.

If we do, then one day as we're standing on the side of that mountain, a heavy rain and a strong wind will come. In other words, our issue with anger or abuse—or whatever has kept us in bondage—will take control of our lives again. We will be swept off the side of that mountain and driven right back into the valley where we've lived so much of our lives in defeat and addiction. After we've repeated that pattern time and time again, we may be too discouraged to even try climbing the mountain again. From that place, it's easy to accept defeat, because we imagine that's how it's going to be for the rest of our lives.

Some people do try to live in that unfinished place. They're still in bondage, but they call it freedom, because they haven't learned that there is a better place for them to live. I believe that there is a mountaintop life for all of us, for every human being upon this earth. But it's not just handed to us. We have to endure. We've got to finish climbing the mountain.

One day, if we're willing, we will make it to the top. Even though we will have experienced pain to get there, the victory will have made it all worthwhile. We'll just be grateful that we didn't give up, that we kept moving forward. Believe me, it's worth the effort.

THE BENEFITS
OF PEOPLE, PLACES & THINGS

CHAPTER SEVEN:

Things to Live By

As we talked about in an earlier chapter, many people who have lived an addictive lifestyle have thrown the wrong things away: education, good jobs, a reasonable place to live. Now it's time to start caring about those things again.

It may start with something as simple as "keeping your room clean." Small steps like these are actually big steps, because they indicate we are moving in a different direction. They remind us that the little things count, and the process of caring about them is an important part of establishing order in our lives.

When your life was going downhill, you missed a lot and threw away a lot. A lot of men in our program missed even a basic high-school education. After they dropped out and watched their class-mates move on to decent jobs and perhaps college, they may have been too embarrassed to return to school. But today there are so many opportunities for older adults to get an education. Several men in our program have learned to read or have improved their basic reading, writing, and math skills. That alone can be a huge encouragement and can help them get better jobs.

But as we go looking for the things we missed, we need to make sure that we're adding good things to our lives as well. What we need are not more things or better things, or even fewer things, necessarily. What we need is thankfulness, and it starts in small ways.

As I've said before, just about every man who comes into our program is initially thankful he's here. He's been given a place to stay, food to eat, people who care about him, and an opportunity to change his life. But it doesn't take long for him to forget those things.

It didn't take more than a month or two for one specific man in our program to start complaining that we wouldn't give him special treatment on the cafeteria line. There were forty men in line to be served, and he was insisting on being served three different types of cereal in the same bowl. Every other man took the bowl that was handed to him, but when this fellow was told he couldn't have what he wanted, he began to get angry with the kitchen staff.

He hadn't complained that he didn't have to live on the street, or that we were taking him back and forth to the hospital to help repair the years of damage from drug and alcohol abuse. He was complaining about a bowl of cereal—not that he didn't have enough, but that he wasn't allowed to have three different types of cereal. In short, he was complaining that he couldn't get his own way.

How easy it is for us to forget where we have come from, but how important it is for us to remember. And we remember by being thankful for the small things.

If we develop gratitude for the small things, we will find that thankfulness becomes a habit—a good habit—in our lives. Our thankfulness can change our perspective on everything and everyone around us, including all the good things and all the wonderful people we have taken for granted.

More Than Ordinary Things

David once had a wife and children. He had worked as a chef in five-star restaurants around the world. He had even been a gardener at the White House. But tragedies in his life hit hard. He started drinking, and eventually he lost everything. For a while at least, he lived in a cardboard box on the street.

When David came to our program he had no confidence. You could see that he was thinking, *How in the world am I going to make it?* Well, we had to work on the foundation, and you probably know what I told him: "I want you to keep your room clean."

I knew he could accomplish that, and I knew he would find success and encouragement in doing it. Few people understand that a major key to overcoming low self-esteem lies in giving someone a simple goal he can accomplish.

Keep your room clean. And after you do that successfully, I'm going to ask you to do something else. But everything I'll ask is something I know you can do. In this way, I'm going to help build your confidence as we look for the issues in your life that need to be addressed.

Each success we have gives us hope for the next challenge. If keeping our room clean or establishing some other basic order in our lives makes a difference, the next step can make an even bigger difference. With enough time and patience and perseverance and grace, we might be able to get our wives and children back. We might be able to get our homes or jobs back. If we can believe for the small things, that's when our journey out of addiction begins.

We might object to having to start at the basics. Sure, it's humbling. But, as I said earlier, we missed some things along the way—things that we really need in order to move forward—and there's no time like the present to go back and get them.

Some people who have life-controlling issues

may not need to start at the most basic level, but most do. For those of us who have lived a life of destruction, it becomes a big thing just to accomplish a little thing—things that most people take for granted.

At The Bridge, the program I've been talking about all through this book, we take what people assumed were the ordinary things of life and make them special again. Once a week, we give each man a five-minute phone call to his family. Do you realize how important that becomes? What was once just an ordinary thing now becomes something of immense significance. What we're really doing is giving him an appreciation for life all over again, letting him see the blessings of his life—maybe for the first time.

Some of you might be wondering, *Why is the phone call so short?* There's a good reason. With about five minutes to talk, the conversation stays focused on what's important. You won't hear the wife going into details about all the problems and the bills. That would be a distraction for her husband in this stage of his growth. They won't be talking about what's going on in the old neighborhood. You know what you'll hear them say?

Honey, I love you so much. I really miss you, and I'm praying for you.

Believe me, the wife wants to talk to him about all the challenges she's facing, but there's just no time. There will come a time, though, when he gets that letter. Then he will hear about those other things: the bills piling up, the children's difficulties in school, the car that needs fixing. Then that same man may come to me and say, "I've got to go home. I can't be here when my wife is going through all of this. I need to be there with her."

There are plenty of things that I don't have the answer for, not just in my life, but in the lives of others, too. That's where I've turned to faith, and that's where I point others.

"You're not going to come out of this situation if you don't also apply faith," I tell him. "You've gone in too deep to just walk out of this on your own. If I don't push you into this area, we're both defeated, because I know my strength can't get you out. My wisdom isn't enough."

Faith is foreign territory to anyone who has lived a life of addiction. We're supposed to be in control. We're supposed to have the answers. Faith is tough for us, because faith is essentially trust, and trust, as we've said before, is something that has been broken so many times in our lives. We don't want to go there again. But my journey of faith has led me to God, and there I have found a trust that has not disappointed me. I don't know how I could have made it without Him.

A lot of people try to hide behind God, as if He

somehow magically takes away all of our responsibility to live right. That's far from the truth. If anything, God places a higher responsibility on us than we have known before. In my life, I have known His strength as I have opened my life up to Him every day.

Walking in Freedom

My freedom from addiction didn't happen quickly. For the first five years or so after I stopped using drugs, I grew in my understanding about addiction and its effects on my life. Over the next few years, I discovered that I had victory over my addiction and over a lot of the old patterns of behavior, but I still thought I would always be in "recovery." Finally, I knew that I was delivered from my addiction.

What do I mean by that? I changed the people, the places, and the things in my life, and as I did, the addictive behavior no longer had control over me. No longer did I have cravings or desires for drugs. No longer were drugs my master. As long as I kept the boundaries around me to have the right people, places, and things in my life, I was free from all of my old bondage.

The amazing thing was that I was just putting into practice something my mother told me a long time ago: "Son, be careful of the people you're around, the places you go, and the things that you allow in your life."

For me, that spells deliverance. The question I have for you is: What is your way out? As I've said before—and I've seen it in my own life as well as in the lives of others—if there was a way in, there is a way out!

After many years of walking in my sobriety, I had an opportunity to attend a Narcotics Anonymous meeting with someone as a way to support them. It was a "closed" meeting, which means that you weren't allowed to attend unless you had an addiction yourself. Each person was given an opportunity to talk about their addiction, and the usual way of beginning was to say, "Hello. I'm William, and I'm a drug addict."

But I couldn't say that and be honest. I had been a drug addict before, and I had admitted it. But now they were asking me to say something that wasn't true. I wasn't an addict any more. I had been delivered.

So when it came time for me to say something, I said something like, "Hello. My name is William Washington, and I've been delivered from drug addiction."

One of the leaders came up to me and said, "You're going to have to leave."

I said, "Why do I have to leave? Because I'm not going to confess that I'm defeated in this? I'm not defeated. About five years ago I would have said that, but not any longer. I have victory over this!"

He just said, "Get out." So I got up and left.

I'm not saying that I'm immune to those old problems in my life, but I will say that I no longer have any craving for the drug, and I was on crack cocaine. That's one of the most addictive substances I know. It's a drug that will defeat you physically, mentally, emotionally, and spiritually. At one time in my life I did almost anything to get the drug. I gave up everything and everyone dear to me. I was an addict all right. But I'm not anymore.

You know, I wasn't born an addict. And now I have the same freedom I once had as a child: I don't wake up with a craving for crack. I don't even think about it. I don't go to a meeting three times a week to confess my weakness to it. I have no desire to go back to that type of lifestyle. And I understand the boundaries that are important for me to continue to enjoy this freedom.

So, even though it is important to confess that we have an addiction—to begin to embrace the truth that will set us free—we don't have to keep confessing it over and over again for the rest of our lives. Because even our addiction can be an excuse to stay in bondage. And by the way, just because you think about the object of your addiction every now and then, it doesn't necessarily mean that it has control over you. With crack, it takes about two years of staying away from it to begin to feel some freedom from the drug. For the majority of people who get high with crack, they just *think* about smoking crack and their body responds as if they're actually smoking it. Only time takes that away, nothing else but time.

Why did they want me to get out of the meeting when I wouldn't say I was an addict? It's because I was a threat to what they believed. They believed that the only way they could stay sober or clean was if they continued to confess their addiction. Now just to be clear, I do believe that meetings like this can provide a lot of help when people are first coming out of an addictive lifestyle. They have their purpose, and a lot of people—even a lot of my friends—have gained significant strength from the support offered through AA and NA.

But when you stop and think about it, it's a little odd to think that the only way I can stay well is by continually admitting I'm sick. Yes, we need to address our physical issues and past abuses. But there is something more. There is freedom, but we will not find it if we allow ourselves to become content just living within a system. I have lived by the things I have been talking about in this book, and I have found freedom and deliverance. No, it didn't happen overnight. I had to go beyond dealing with just my addiction to deal with those deeper issues, the dark places that had controlled my life and fueled my addiction.

If you need to, keep attending your NA or AA meeting, but don't stop there, not if you want to go back to a place of true freedom from the object of your addiction, back to a time before you took your first drink or smoked your first joint. Recovery starts the day you say you're not going to take a drink. Deliverance is a place of freedom where you no longer have to confess your weakness to drugs or alcohol. It's a place of victory. Recovery should lead to deliverance, but most people settle for recovery.

From my experience, they're settling for far too little.

The Process of Deliverance

If you've gotten away from the object of your addiction for a while, you're probably ready to move on to that next big goal. But remember, few people can reach their goals overnight with one giant step. More often than not, it's a process, and we need to learn some things along the way. Then, when we reach that place of total deliverance, we can look back and realize what we've been delivered from. (We will also know what we've been delivered to—in other words, where we're going.)

I was speaking with a counselor recently on this topic. I told him that one of the men in our program had been delivered from a sexual addiction, and I wanted him to receive counseling.

"I don't understand," the counselor said. "Why does he need counseling if he has been delivered from it?"

"Because," I replied, "I want him to know what he has been delivered from."

Even though we may be experiencing success, if we do not understand what we have been delivered from, we are likely to make the same mistakes as in the past. More than anything else, it's important for us to go through the *process* of deliverance. We need to know where our struggles have been, not just for our addiction, but for the attitudes and behaviors that have fed our addiction.

What situations make us tense? When do we tend to get angry? What makes us impatient? As we begin to understand what we've been set free from, we can set up boundaries in our lives. Without these boundaries, before we know it, we can be right back in our addiction and wonder how we got there.

When I look at my lifestyle and the freedom I have now, this is what it means to me: I look at my family. I see the joy and peace in their lives. My children don't have to worry about their father not showing up, or that he will take the mortgage money and spend it on drugs. I am thankful that I have money in my checkbook to be able to provide the material things they need. My wife sleeps peacefully at night. No longer is she sitting on the sofa until one or two o'clock in the morning to see if I'm coming home or who might be coming home with me.

But I also know what I've been delivered from: my father's abuse, poverty, homelessness, and the insecurity that comes with it. I cannot be the man I am today without knowing who I was and where I've come from. Just because my father rejected me didn't mean that I wasn't good enough. The past events of our lives—like the hurt and abuse that we have lived through—can lie to us and tell us that things cannot change, and because we are hurting, it's easy to believe those lies. Some people might think I'm talking about having self-pity, but I'm not. I'm talking about facing the reality that the pain hurt, that it wasn't just a physical wound, but that it was also a spiritual wound. That's important. We can't just put medicine on or apply counseling to our wounds. We need a spiritual solution as well.

I've been through the process—day in, day out—for the last seventeen years or so. That doesn't mean I'm perfect; it means I understand that I'm not perfect and that I still have a long way to go.

When I see people who are just beginning to walk away from an addiction, and are setting very high goals, I know that they may be just setting themselves up for failure. They are trying to look past the process directly to the goal; they are trying to take one, two, or three huge leaps from the starting line to the finish. But that's not how you run a race. You can't get where you're going without pacing yourself and learning how to run the race correctly. Again, it's in the process that you learn what you've been delivered *from* and what you've been delivered *to*—one day at a time.

That's why we ask the men in our program to make a commitment for eighteen months. Every day brings a challenge to be faithful in the small things, and I believe that the small things are crucial. I would even say that they are more important than the "big" things.

There's an old saying that "the little foxes spoil the vines." In other words, the little things—the things that seem insignificant—are the things that can ruin the bigger picture for us. It's important to be faithful in the little commitments we make, such as being on time to work. We can say, "Well, I was only two or three minutes late." But we were still late, and that two or three minutes can turn into five or ten, then fifteen. The next thing you know, you're not showing up at all. It's always the small things that lead us back into a place of drinking or using drugs. If we take care of the small things, we won't have to worry about the bigger things that might trip us up.

Of course, no one is perfect. But we need to

seek what is right and true, and be the best we can be, being honest even in our weaknesses. People who don't understand a lifestyle of addiction may look at you sometimes and say, "Don't you think you're being a little too hard on yourself? People make mistakes. They have challenges."

That's all true. But if those of us with patterns of addiction-related behavior start thinking that we don't have to take care of the "small things," we will not get out of our addiction; we will go deeper into it.

When I was working in that auto-body shop many years ago, my boss told me that it was the little things that would ruin the job. He said, "William, when the workman pulls that car out of the bay, ninety percent of that car is going to look great. I wouldn't hire him unless he could paint well or get the dents out of a car the right way.

"What you have to pay attention to are the smaller things. Are the door jambs and edges painted properly? Is there enough clear finish on top of the paint? Are the bolts—the ones you can't see unless you get under the car—put back properly?"

He told me that if the little things on the car were done right, the job would be completed well, according to our standards and also the customer's. Again, if we take care of the little things in our lives, the big things—like staying away from drugs and alcohol, getting into a life of crime, and all the rest—will be taken care of, too.

Take the small steps to success. Do the next thing in front of you, even if it is a simple act of serving someone else. It may seem as if you're not going anywhere, but you'll be building an important part of your foundation for the new life ahead of you.

Response-Ability

If there were ever any reasons to walk away from our responsibilities, the patterns of our addictive behavior seemed to offer them to us. We were experts at using excuses to avoid the consequences of our irresponsible actions.

More than that, for a lot of reasons—including our tendency not to think through our decisions carefully—we found ourselves having to react to our circumstances. We felt like victims, unaware that our own poor choices had created the difficult circumstances we were in.

But as we continue to grow in our victory over the lifestyle of addiction, we realize that we're now able to respond to situations instead of just react. We have an opportunity to think and plan. And the first part of those plans should be to take responsibility for what we have done. As I often put it to the men in our program: The path you walked to get here is the same path you need to walk to get out.

When I first began my walk out of an addictive lifestyle, I owed something close to $90,000, and my take-home pay was a little more than $156 a week. After mandatory payments for child support and restitution, I was left with about $63 for groceries, gas, rent, and so on for the next seven days. In some ways it would have been easy to take one of the suggestions several people were offering: file for bankruptcy or go back to selling drugs.

Instead, I sought extra work at night detailing cars, a skill for which I had been professionally trained. Somehow, week by week, we made it. I put into practice the things I have been talking about in this book, and I didn't give up. When I got home from work, I went to work at my second job. No longer was I willing to depend on other people to take care of me. My wife and I even decided it would be better if we stopped accepting the government's aid for dependent children. It seemed crazy from a financial standpoint, but I really believed that the government's help was discouraging me from accepting full responsibility for where we were financially.

It took several years for us to get out of debt, but we did it. My wife and I own our own home now, and we don't worry about our next meal.

Today when I look at my family's needs or the needs of the men's program, I am confident that there will be a way of provision. When the money doesn't show up, I don't resort to doing crazy things or flying into a panic. I have been through the process of seeing God's faithfulness. I've taken it one step at a time, and it's brought a wonderful confidence—a very real faith—into my everyday life.

Looking Back

Of course, some of the debts we owe don't have anything to do with money. I know—from listening to the men we serve as well as looking back on my own life—that we have hurt people in many different ways.

There is a blessing in taking responsibility for the harm we've done, for the debts we owe. It may not be easy, but it's the right thing to do. Taking responsibility not only blesses others, but it also begins to break the cycle of addiction-related behavior within us.

One challenge we face as we address the hurt we have caused other people is our own blindness. We see the problems in other people's lives more easily than we see our own. I think that's true for just about everybody, but especially for someone who has been hurt deeply and repeatedly. The hurt is so prevalent in our own lives, we readily feel the pain that others cause us. But it's harder for us to see the pain and hurt we cause others.

When I first started walking into a new lifestyle, I focused my energies on getting off drugs, but I never seriously worked on the pain I had brought to others. I found myself overlooking those aspects of my past, because I didn't want to take a look at the real me. In particular, I had to face the way I had treated my wife and family. My lack of respect for them had become a big part of my addiction and the behavior patterns of that addiction.

I worked through a lot of those issues over time, but it wasn't until several years later, when I started writing a book about my life and the beginnings of The Bridge, that I came face to face with a lot more of the pain in my life. There were things from my childhood that I had pushed down inside of me and decided I would never deal with.

Much of the pain had come from my father. At times he had beaten my mother until she was unconscious. He had physically abused me, too. Besides that, I lived in a community filled with violence; every week we witnessed a shoot-out or a fight where someone was seriously hurt or killed.

These were the things I had to revisit in order to share a piece of my life in my first book, *His Grace Is Sufficient*. And when I opened that door for these things to come to the surface, I found myself reliving the pain all over again. I had never been healed from that lifestyle, from the abuse.

It is so important for us to return to and

address the things that have controlled our lives and kept us in bondage. It was not an easy step for me to take, but at the end of that journey, I was at a better place than I had ever been with my father and my past. One morning I woke up and felt liberated; I felt lightened.

I'm not saying that all of that hurt was gone. But I had faced some of my deepest pain, and by the grace of God, I had come through it and was better for having done so. The same can happen for you, too. God intended for every one of us to live a life of freedom. And He gives us the courage to go through whatever we need to go through in order to get there.

Again, revisiting our pain and learning to express it is not something we do in isolation. Isolating ourselves from others was part of what initially got us into trouble, or at least got us deeper into trouble. Take Martin, for example.

Everyone who knew Martin thought he had it made: nice home, beautiful wife, etc. But inside, Martin was miserable. He never was able to let the people who admired him know how wounded he really felt, so when he fell back into his old pattern of addiction, he sought out the people on the streets. They would listen and not criticize. Though they made up only a small portion of his circle of friends and acquaintances, their influence encouraged him to make the bad choices that landed him in jail time and time again.

By the way, Martin was someone who knew all the "right things" in terms of handling his addiction. In fact, he had been through some of the best programs for life-controlling issues and was even a highly recommended leader. He knew the principles; he just didn't walk them out. He hadn't established boundaries to keep him away from his own problem areas. And, as I said, he wasn't willing to revisit the pain of his past and open up to the people who cared about him.

I believe most people stay in bondage because they don't know how to be honest. They feel separated from people, even from those who are closest to them. So they hold in their feelings or their wrong desires. But they can't hold them in forever. Eventually, a circumstance or a crisis will force some of their life-controlling issues to the surface. If they don't start working with these issues in their lives, it will keep taking away from the things they were meant to enjoy. For some it may end in divorce, broken relationships, or even jail.

So I encourage you to take a look into your own places of challenge, that the testimony of my success might also be yours.

What About You?

Each of us has our own particular issues to

identify when it comes to our addictive lifestyle. At The Bridge, we assist every man as he personally goes through that process, but I realize that most of you will never be in a program like The Bridge. What do you do? How do you go back to the basics? What does "keeping your room clean" mean for you?

The fact is, unless you have accountability—accountability that you are willing to take seriously—you're likely not to change at all. It has to be a team effort. When people leave The Bridge, they have the same choices to make as you: They can return to the old ways of defeat and bondage, or they can choose life. I had more accountability than most people I know, and I don't believe I would have made it otherwise. I'll talk a little bit more about that in the next chapter, but everyone in my life who cared about me, who prayed for me, who loved me and encouraged me and challenged me was a blessing. (If you're reading this, I can't thank you enough.)

So what are you going to do? If you choose to embrace positive change, I can almost guarantee you that there are a lot of people—especially those in your family and those friends who understand what you are going through—waiting in the wings to give you the support you need.

STAYING ON TRACK

CHAPTER EIGHT:

Don't Give Up

If you have begun to walk away from your addictive lifestyle, keep walking. It is a journey that will bring you many surprises. There will be healing in your life you never expected, but there will also be some difficulties you didn't count on.

I've said it before in different ways throughout this book: The path that got you into your bondage is the same path you've got to travel to get out of your bondage. That's what stops a lot of people in their tracks. They want to move on with a fresh start, but you can't move forward with confidence until you know what you've been delivered from. Some of the issues *we* need to address are a reality not because we have done wrong, but because *others* have done wrong to us. Unless you understand the danger zones of people, places, and things, you'll be tripping over them all along the way.

Remember, sometimes the things you're fighting

against are the very things God wants to use to bring you healing and deliverance. Don't turn back when the truth starts to reveal painful places in your life. People who love you will say things that challenge you, but that doesn't mean they are saying them because they want to hurt you. Lies and deceit have been such a huge part of your life, you may have forgotten what the truth feels like.

This battle is about more than an addiction. It's about a lifestyle that perhaps led to or fed an addiction. It's about healing the wounds of the past that made you want to hide within that addiction. If you've stopped engaging in the addiction, that's great, but don't let that be the only measure of your success. Lasting change and healing will probably take time.

Another Word for Friends and Families

Some people experience an immediate freedom from their addiction when they surrender their lives to God. That is a wonderful gift. It was not my experience, but I know that it happens.

In our program, The Bridge, we do not even talk about a man's addiction until after the first several months of his time with us. Instead, we go after the addictive behaviors that have fueled and supported the addiction; we bring to light the life-controlling issues.

We need to detox ourselves from the lifestyle—

from the people, places, and things that have contributed to our addictive patterns—even more than we need to detox ourselves from the drug or other object of our addiction.

So while it is a wonderful thing if a person has experienced an immediate freedom from the craving for his or her addiction, that is only part of the answer.

As we've talked about before, there are people—often parents and sometimes wives—who try to shield their loved ones from the consequences of their addiction. In the past, they were the ones who made the phone calls to say their son or husband was sick and couldn't come to work, or hired a good lawyer, or made excuses for the behavior. None of that worked because the addictive behavior continued to fuel the addiction, and the problem just got worse. What seemed like care and concern turned out to just enable the addict to continue being an addict.

There was a young man, Stephen, who was in our program not long ago. He had been through plenty of programs, and he was at ours as an alternative to a jail sentence. Like everyone else, he made an eighteen-month commitment.

For the first six months, Stephen was a model student. He had been through a state program while he was incarcerated, and he had learned how to give all the right answers, how to hide his true self.

After six months, we received notice from the parole board that Stephen's jail time was over. Now, he was free to go, except that he had made an eighteen-month commitment to us. He came and told me that he had heard from God and that it was time for him to leave. I'm sure he thought that would be the kind of language that would "register" with me because I am a pastor.

I questioned him: "You have heard from God that it's time to leave, and yet you don't have a job, you don't have a place to live? Your parents don't think it's a good idea, and yet they are the ones you are going to ask to support you?"

None of what I said mattered to him. He had already made up his mind. And when it came time to leave the property, do you know who picked him up? His girlfriend. She was the one he had lied to and deceived for so long. She was the one who would continue to support his addiction. Like everyone who enables an addict, she would do it to her own hurt as well.

For a man to successfully go through the process of recovery and deliverance, that type of enabling has to be challenged and removed. Why should he change at all if he can keep living in bondage with a little bit of help? I know that family and friends don't see it this way. They only see their loved one in pain. But stepping back—even giving them room to fail—is a necessary part of their healing.

Learning to Forgive

Every single one of us has had an imperfect life. In one way or another, we have been mistreated, misunderstood, or disrespected. But as we mentioned earlier, we can't let our past difficulties become our present excuses. We need to look at the difficulties of our past as experiences that present us with an opportunity.

Let's start with something simple: *I grew up in a poor neighborhood*. First, that gave you the advantage of understanding a much-neglected and misunderstood part of our society. Second, it may have given you the motivation to do something better with your life. Third, you may have an opportunity to reach back into that neighborhood and make a difference.

I don't want to make light of your pain. I'm sure that some of you have been through more than I can imagine. Yet even in those situations, however dark they have been, you can find hope. Even our most difficult past events can be turned around and used in our favor. Our suffering has the potential to produce compassion; as we find comfort, we may also give comfort to others.

None of the places we have been—nothing that has happened to us—has the power to hold us permanently in its grasp. There is a way out of those places. There is a way out of the bondage of our past.

I remember when I first began to deal with the

hurt I had experienced at the hands of my father. I was growing in my experience of faith in a heavenly Father, and I was developing a personal relationship with Him. As I grew secure in that relationship, I was able to look at my childhood in a different light. I knew that my heavenly Father expected me to forgive my earthly father.

As long as I refused to forgive my father, it kept me in bondage. It kept hatred, distrust, and dishonesty within me. His abuse had left those things in my life. Until I forgave him, I couldn't get rid of them. I couldn't be free myself until I set him free through forgiveness.

It was a process. Even when I chose to consciously forgive him, old thoughts would return at unexpected moments, and they would challenge me to hold a grudge, to remain bitter. Each time those thoughts came back, I had a choice to forgive or to hold on to my hurt.

Many years passed. My father and I had no relationship until one day I got a call that he was dying. We took him into our home for a while and nurtured him back to health. My father and I had some good conversations during those days.

Imagine if I had held on to the hurt and abuse I had suffered at his hands. I would never have had the chance to rebuild our relationship. My children would never have known their grandfather. As I opened my heart to my father in forgiveness, it gave him the strength to deal with his own addiction, and I learned a lot of things about my father that I had never known.

He had been abused, too. Like me, he had left home at fifteen, and he was fifteen when he married my mother. He loved her dearly, but he also married her as an escape from the abuse he was receiving from his own father. My father started drinking to cover up the hurt from that abuse, and he continued drinking to escape the overwhelming responsibility of being a husband and father at age fifteen.

When my father's drinking started, he began to abuse others in the same way he had been abused. He abused my mother verbally as well as physically. When this happened, the next morning I would look at the bruises on my mother's face and arms, and I would ask her why my father abused her. Her response would be, "Times are hard for your father, but it will get better." But it never did.

My father's addiction caused a lot of pain to others, but it also kept him in constant bondage. When he woke at 5 a.m., he would go into the kitchen to get a cold glass of water to have with his first drink of alcohol. I was only six years old, and unless I got up early with him, I might not see him at all that day because of his work schedule. I loved him, and I wanted to be around him. Getting that glass of water every morning became my "little job" for him. That was my joy. I didn't see his bondage to the bottle: In order to function for the day, he had to drink at least a pint of liquor before he left for work.

Every morning, too, I remember watching my mother at the stove cooking his breakfast, and afterward she would make his lunch. She would start by making him a couple of sandwiches, and then she began another morning ritual. She would take the thermos out of his lunch box and replace it with a fifth of bourbon. (Yes, it was my father who was the example of the functioning addict I spoke about earlier in this book.)

It's easy to come to a quick judgment about my father. But the point here—and the reason I've been writing this book—is to describe how the bondage, the hurt, the pain, and the life-controlling issues all fueled the addiction so that my father's life was out of control. I'm sad to say it didn't get better; it got worse.

I've given you a lot to absorb here, but I want you to know that when I'm talking about forgiveness, I'm dealing with far more than shallow issues. The wounds in my life were deep and personal, but by the grace of God, I learned how to release those hurts. So while I learned a lot about my father while he was living in our home, more important, a lot of old wounds in my life were healed.

I'm not saying that all of my past wounds are completely gone; some things take a long time to heal. But my father and I had a different relationship after it was all over, and I had learned a little bit more about not making excuses and about how to forgive. The steps I have been sharing with you in this book have brought me to a place of freedom in this area of my life, which can be true for you as well.

A Word About Leadership

Often, when people began to feel the first taste of freedom from their addictive behavior, they want to immediately begin helping others. That's natural. We've found freedom from a nightmare. Let's share the good news.

The problem is that, in the beginning, we only know the first part of the story. We have yet to learn how to press forward through the challenging situations before us. We're still in the honeymoon phase. Of course there are many things we can say and do to help others, but at this point it's easy to transfer our addiction to the "role of leadership."

I say the "role of leadership," because to develop real leadership takes time; it's a process. If you're faithful in a little, you'll be given more.

The temptation to take on the role of leadership too early is sometimes complicated by existing leaders who see a gifted person coming out of addiction. Some leaders are looking for men who have a gift to help other men become good fathers and husbands. Because they are so eager to see this particular gift actively used, leaders may sometimes put a gifted man in a position of authority for which he is not yet ready. In other words, instead of developing the man—and the gift within that man—they overlook the man's need and put him in a role of leadership before that man has a proper foundation for leadership.

That's a good way to end the effectiveness of that gift, at least for the time being. No one should be leading others when he has life-controlling issues of his own for which he still needs leadership. A man in that position is almost guaranteed to fall. And when he falls, his fall will affect many more people.

I am thankful that my former pastor didn't let that happen to me. As I was walking out of my addiction, I received a lot of invitations from churches to speak, but he wouldn't let me accept any of them for about the first two years. The only place he would let me speak publicly was the local jail. It felt as if I had shackles on my feet, but I needed that restraint, and I'm glad I submitted to it. Those invitations were still there after two years, and there have been many more since.

That's why it's important for those of us who are coming out of a life of addiction to stay focused on our own lives for at least two years before we go out and try to help others. During those first two years, we are given an opportunity to put into practice what we have been taught. We will learn things that we didn't read in a book or hear in a meeting, important lessons that will give us strength to face the challenges ahead. Many times there will be pressure for us to move into leadership, but we can't base our decision on the need others have for our gifts. We need to consider, and be honest about, the addictive behavior that we are still working to change.

Remember, all of us are called to serve. But if you are put in a place of leadership and become an example for others before you are ready, you are probably setting yourself up for failure. Be patient, and be willing to respond to the challenges in your life today. Then, when the opportunity for leadership does arrive, you will be ready.

Accountability

When you are coming out of a lifestyle of addiction, you need to spend time with people who are willing to be honest with you. But they also need to know how and when to bring up the important issues. They need to have a certain level of understanding about addiction, and your addiction in particular, so that you can't get away with deceiving those people as you have in the past.

Early on in the process of recovery and deliverance from my addiction, I was part of a "house group" at my church. We would meet together to get to know each other better, to pray, and to study the Bible. I got a lot out of that group, and I knew that everyone there cared about me.

While I was able to share some of the issues I was going through, I never felt fully free to express myself. I wasn't sure any of them would understand. I was dying inside, though on the outside I gave the appearance that everything was fine. I needed someone who understood my addiction, and I found that understanding by starting to befriend men who had come out of a life of addiction and were having success in their recovery. I began to talk to them about the life I had come from, and the life I wanted to live. Years later, as I looked deeper, I discovered at least one man who had experienced success in his deliverance from addiction, and I sought him out for friendship.

The men who come into our program have many different issues, and some of them we don't have answers for. I can sit down and talk with them to a certain extent, but I personally have never dealt with some of their issues. So I seek out a group that can minister to these men, people who have lived through a certain issue and found victory from it, and people who have lived in that victory for a number of years.

So I would encourage you to get around people who can help build that structure in your life. From that, with hard work and discipline, you'll learn that it's possible to live not only in recovery, but also in deliverance.

Of course you don't need to completely surround yourself with people who have addiction-related issues, but make sure you have someone you can call when the times get tough. That individual needs to be not only strong enough to speak encouragement into your life, but also willing to correct you when necessary.

A Word and Example for Accountability Partners

Holding someone accountable, even with their permission, is not an easy responsibility. A person coming out of a life of addiction has had experience with using many "weapons" that make accountability difficult: making excuses, pretending everything is fine, outright lying, and anger.

Anger is a weapon that can effectively keep others away from us. At The Bridge, there have been times when a man gets very angry. He may just be expressing himself in a violent manner, or he may want to physically fight someone. Often, a group of men will gather around him and try to calm him down.

Early on in the history of the program, I considered that sort of anger as a reason to dismiss a man. Now, however, I understand that he is just using one of the weapons from his past, a weapon that has successfully (he thinks) kept people from hurting him. I know that the issue can't be addressed while he is in front of the other men, that we will need to have a place where we can talk.

"Just move away from him," I tell those who are standing around.

Then I'll turn to that man and say, "Come on into my office."

Once we're there, and he's had a little time to calm down, I'll look him straight in the eyes.

"Look," I'll say. "I am not the one who hurt you. I wasn't the one who abandoned you." I'll remind him that we were the ones who took him in, who are trying to help him. "Have we ever treated you unfairly or done you wrong?"

That's the first part of what I want him to hear, but the second part is important, too.

"Your anger does not intimidate me. You cannot come on this property and disrespect me, the other men, and this program."

What I am trying to do is set the boundaries of respect, and also let this man know that I am not against him. My heart is to help him. I want to be honest when I'm frustrated, but I want to express it in a way that will be an example to him.

"These are some of the tools you have used to keep people away from you. You have been using these weapons to keep you from listening and from receiving," I say. "You need to take these defenses down. They are something you use to try to protect a very broken, very wounded man— wounded from the things others have done to you, and wounded from the things you have done to yourself."

These conversations may go on for about thirty minutes or more, and you may be surprised to learn that most of the men will break down and cry. They have been looking for someone strong enough to stand up to them.

An outburst of anger is not a time to run away from someone who has struggled with an addiction. It's then that he needs you the most. (There may come a time that you need to back away, if only for a while. You don't want to endanger your own safety, and you will have to exercise good judgment.)

Often, people walking out of a life of addiction need the counsel of someone who has experienced their particular type of problem. But other times, they just need someone who will "be there," someone who will be strong enough not to give up in their time of need.

Religious Cover-Up

I remember observing a group of former drug and alcohol addicts who were living and working in a Christian ministry. My first impression of them was that they were so polite. They were some of the nicest people I had ever met, but as I observed them for a while, I realized that their "good manners" were another tool to cover up their addiction. Let me explain.

It's easy to see that a man has problems when he explodes with anger. But there is another cover-up: being polite, saying the right things, and keeping up appearances. This cover-up holds just as much potential for destruction. Addiction is always trying to find a place to hide and make itself seem normal. That's why it takes people who have been there to understand some of the deeper issues and patterns of addiction.

Many addicts live with a wonderful set of principles. They can tell you all about what they need to do to be changed, but they are living in defeat. They have a tremendous knowledge about people, places, and things, but they are not willing to apply it. They may even have embraced some of the truth of the Bible for their lives, yet they are still living in the same bondage. I have seen this result over and over again from programs that teach a man "the answers" without giving him an opportunity to live the truth for himself.

Learning to live by a set of rules is not going to set us free. Without a spiritual power at work in our hearts to change us, even the best programs can become just another set of principles that no one has the strength to live out or sustain. They can become another type of prison, almost like another addiction. Our lives may show signs of structure and order; we may even be able to stay away from drugs or alcohol for a long period of time. But we won't have the kind of life that freedom and deliverance brings.

What we need is true spiritual strength and solid principles working together. We have to face the deeper issues in our lives, issues that we know we cannot face in our own strength. As we learn to rely on a power greater than ourselves, we begin to discover freedom from our past bondage. For me, that requires a personal relationship with God through Jesus Christ. As I grow in this relationship, I also grow in the strength to live out the principles I learn from others and read in the Bible. Only then am I able to walk in deliverance, both physically and spiritually.

And from what I'm learning, that's what real change is all about.

A New Name

Sometimes the blessings or challenges we face can change our name. That name may come from a job where we find our identity. Or it may be based on the tragedies and hurt we have faced, names like "drug-addict" or "abuser."

But the good news is this: Those names can be changed. I have changed some of the more challenging names in my life by facing them, and by allowing my relationship with God to give me a new name. The name God gives us is a vision for who He sees us to be. In His eyes, we are that person already. They are the eyes of faith, seeing early glimpses of strength and hope in our lives and believing there is more to come.

But God also has a process to help us become that person He sees us to be. It's the process of trials and difficulties, because the root of change starts on the inside. And we move through those trials in His strength, not ours. As one first-century writer expressed it, suffering produces perseverance, perseverance produces character, and character produces hope. Hope allows us to endure through the difficult times. It keeps us looking forward. It helps us stay focused. And it will not disappoint us.

So find hope. Find it in the people, places, and things with which you surround your life. Find it in the positive decisions and progress you've already made. But most of all, find your hope in God. He is the only firm foundation for your hope, and he alone can see you through to deliverance.

Don't give up just because you don't see change on the first day, or the third, or the thirtieth. Remember, it's going to take time for change to be evident in your life. If one thing doesn't work, try something else. There are a lot of people who have been trapped in a lifestyle of addiction and who have come out of it.

It's happened for me, and I know it can happen for you.

As I look back over my life and see all the pitfalls and challenges on the way, I remember that day when I tried to end my life. I saw no way to get out of the mess I was in and live a productive life. I felt so defeated. I came to a place where my life was of no more value than the gas I had just inhaled or the pills I had swallowed.

But the good news was that there was something there that I could not see. I could not put my hands on it physically. But it was there, waiting for the opportunity to reveal itself to me. That was my God—a God of mercy and grace, a God who would come into my life and establish a fatherhood for me that I did not receive from my own father. He was a God who helped me work on the hurt and pain and rejection that was so deep within me that I felt I was not even worthy to be called "son."

All of that didn't happen in a single moment. It took place step by step. The next day, when the pills and the gas didn't take my life, I woke up to a new beginning. A friend began to talk about this God who could help me. From that, I came to a place where I knew that God could not only help me in my immediate needs but also change my life.

Today, my wife and I have twenty-two years of commitment to each other. We have a daughter at Liberty University and a son at West Point Prep. We have another son in a private military school whose goal is to go to the University of North Carolina. We have another son and another daughter who have graduated from high school and are moving on with their lives, and we are proud of each one of them. This family that seemed to be on a path of destruction now has a testimony that is leading others into a place of hope.

Friends, this testimony is not just for me; it is also for you. Whatever challenges you're going through, whatever mountain you feel that you cannot climb, I'm living proof that through God all things are possible. But there's some work to do. There's some work to do *in* you—to deal with the inner, spiritual issues. And there's some work to do *on* you—to make you into a blessing for your family and your community.

Still, this testimony is for you: a testimony of hope, of love, of another opportunity, of another chance. It belongs to you today.

My challenge to you is that whatever goal you

embrace for your recovery and deliverance, accomplish it. Commit your strength and zeal not just for a moment, but also for a lifetime. When you come to the hard places, know that on the other side your testimony will be, "I've made it to this first place; I can make it to the next."

What you read here is not an illusion or something so far away that you cannot put your hands on it. This can be the testimony of your life or of someone in your family. Regardless of the challenges, the opportunity for change is still here and available today.